TEXAS
AGGIE
MEDALS
OF
HONOR

NUMBER 132:

WILLIAMS-FORD

TEXAS A&M UNIVERSITY

MILITARY HISTORY

SERIES

TEXAS AGGIE MEDALS OF HONOR

SEVEN HEROES OF WORLD WAR II

JAMES R. WOODALL

with a Foreword by James F. Hollingsworth

★

TEXAS A&M UNIVERSITY PRESS
College Station

This paper meets the requirements of
ANSI/NISO z39.48–1992 (Permanence of Paper).
Binding materials have been chosen for durability.

Library of Congress Cataloging-in-Publication Data
Woodall, James R., 1929–
Texas Aggie Medals of Honor : seven heroes of World
War II / James R. Woodall ; with a foreword by James F.
Hollingsworth. – 1ST ed.
p. cm. – (Williams-Ford Texas A&M University military
history series ; no. 132)
Includes bibliographical references and index.
ISBN-13: 978-1-60344-204-6 (cloth : alk. paper)
ISBN-13: 978-1-62349-045-4 (pbk. : alk. paper)
ISBN-13: 978-1-60344-253-4 (e-book)
1. Medal of Honor—Biography. 2. Texas A&M University —
Students — Biography. 3. World War, 1939–1945 — Medals.
4. World War, 1939–1945 — Biography. 5. United States — Armed Forces —
Biography. 6. Heroes — Awards. 7. Heroes — Texas — Biography.
8. Texas — Biography. I. Title. II. Title: Seven heroes of World War II.
III. Series: Williams-Ford Texas A&M University military
history series ; no. 132.
UB434.T4W66 2010
355.1'342 – dc22
2010002451

Unless otherwise indicated, all maps are courtesy Anne Boykin.

This book is dedicated to the
Texas Aggie Corps of Cadets,
past, present, and future.

CONTENTS
★ ★ ★

LIST OF MAPS

★ ★ ★

FOREWORD

★ ★ ★

Col. James Woodall's insightful story of the seven Texas Aggies awarded the Medal of Honor in World War II is very timely and relevant to today's world. Aggies have a distinguished record of service to their country, and the men portrayed in this book exemplify the finest qualities and dedication of the tens of thousands of men and women who have served and are serving our country in times of peace and war. The seven recipients of the Medal of Honor, whose lives and deeds are detailed in this book, have also been honored in other ways at Texas A&M University and in their hometowns.

Using university and military records, interviews with family and friends, and letters and documents, the author has presented a comprehensive portrait of each individual. The history and organization of each one's military unit provides the reader the background necessary to understand the conditions and the battle in which the heroic deed was performed and to comprehend the meaning of the nation's highest award for valor, the Medal of Honor.

A unique aspect of the book is inclusion of information on repatriation and burial of the fallen heroes. Where most battle accounts list wounded and dead, the author has researched what happened after the recipient became a casualty. Five were killed in action, and four of those were eventually returned to the States to their final resting place; one was interred in Italy in accordance with his previously announced wish. Two of the recipients of the Medal of Honor received grievous wounds and spent many months recovering in military hospitals before they could return to civilian life. All exemplify the personal courage, valor, commitment, and determination of those who have fought and served our country.

The author also corrects some erroneous information that appeared in earlier books about the battles and the Medal of Honor recipients and that has often been repeated in subsequent publications. This is a book that needed to be written and that needs to be read, not only by Texas Aggies but also by those interested in American military history as well as those interested in achieving an understanding and appreciation of the full dimensions of humanism, patriotism, and sacrifice.

JAMES F. HOLLINGSWORTH, Class of 1940
Lieutenant General, U.S. Army, Retired

PREFACE

★ ★ ★

Each time I visit the Sam Houston Sanders Corps of Cadets Center on the campus of Texas A&M University, I always pause at the displays of the Turney Leonard and Eli Whiteley Medals of Honor. It is my way of showing respect for these two Aggie heroes. One was a young man in the prime of his life who died bravely in the Huertgen Forest in 1944. The other was a courageous infantry soldier who survived the war and returned to Texas A&M University to become a professor of agronomy.

The Corps Center contains a large bronze bas-relief plaque for each of the seven Texas Aggies awarded the Medal of Honor. On one of my visits, I looked at the plaques and wondered about the other five recipients. Where were the medals for George D. Keathley, Horace S. Carswell, Thomas W. Fowler, William G. Harrell, and Lloyd H. Hughes? Were they in local museums somewhere, in frames hanging on someone's wall, or in boxes stored in a relative's home? Do the owners realize the importance and value of these medals? Do they know how much it would mean to the Aggie community to have the medals displayed in the Corps Center?

I thought someone should have located the medals years earlier. The stories of those brave men should be told in the center too, and I realized that the window of opportunity to gather them was rapidly closing. After all, the medals had been awarded for actions that occurred more than sixty years ago.

The bookstores in College Station are full of books related to Texas A&M University. There are books on school history, traditions, the mascot, Aggie football, good bull stories, Aggies in military service, and even Aggie cookbooks. But where is the book on our Medal of Honor heroes? The seven Aggie Medal of Honor recipients are mentioned in some books, though usually in only a few paragraphs. Up to this point, they have been a footnote to history. Some of the published information is incorrect, and the erroneous material has been repeated in subsequent publications.

So began my quest, a personal project to locate the five Medals of Honor not on display in the Corps Center. The project was not sanctioned by the authorities at Texas A&M University — in fact I told no one at the university. The only official contact I planned was to inform the commandant of cadets once I located a medal, hoping he would follow up and make an effort to arrange for its display in the center.

My first action was to visit the archives at the university library, where I was surprised to find very little information that would assist in the search. (The research papers used in the writing of this book are now housed in the university archives.) I then visited the Association of Former Students to look through past issues of the *Texas Aggie* magazine and found some information of value in locating relatives.

During World War II, 16.5 million men and women served in the U.S. military. The Medal of Honor was awarded to 464 brave men, a ratio of one medal for each 35,560 Americans who served. Among these were 20,000 Texas Aggies, seven of whom received the Medal of Honor, a ratio of one medal for each 2,857 who served. Why the difference? Was it a result of the training in the Corps of Cadets, from which a freshman developed mental toughness and learned to deal with stressful situations? Perhaps it had something to do with the type of young men, mostly from rural areas and small towns, who elected to attend the all-male military college. Maybe George Sessions Perry had it right when he said in his book *The History of Texas A&M,* "Its all-male, military-barracks life has given its boys the salty, free-swinging camaraderie which so often springs up among men disassociated from women." Most likely it was a combination of the above, but this is a subject better addressed by social scientists.

The ultimate purpose of this book is to tell the story of each of the seven Medal of Honor recipients as accurately and in as much depth as possible, preserving their stories for future Aggies. It expands on the wartime service of each individual, telling the story of his military unit and the larger battle in which his actions earned the medal. The chapters also document how each man was honored after the war.

The word "hero" has become a commonplace epitaph often used to describe people who perform unusual acts. The worst abuse is in the media, where the term is used too often and too loosely. The stories of the seven Aggies in this book give the reader a look at authentic heroes.

Many people may be unaware of the significance of the award of a Medal of Honor. To better understand what this represents, the history of the medal is given in chapter two. The stories are presented chronologically by the date of the event for which the medal was awarded.

ACKNOWLEDGMENTS

★ ★ ★

Several people made significant contributions to the production of this book.

I am deeply indebted to those I interviewed or who shared their letters, photographs, manuscripts, and other memorabilia. In particular, I note Rebecca Ann Jordan, the niece of Lt. Lloyd H. "Pete" Hughes and an advocate for securing her uncle's Medal of Honor for display at the Corps Center. She also provided essential information for locating the Thomas W. Fowler Medal of Honor and willingly gave considerable genealogical support in researching the Medal of Honor recipients.

Many people at Texas A&M University provided much kind and essential assistance to me. Don Carter, the university's registrar, provided invaluable information about each recipient, which was vital in reconstructing the story of their early lives and college days. The wonderful people of the Sam Houston Sanders Corps of Cadets Center, including Jeff Gardner, Christy Sparkman, Linda Hawes, Cathy McWhorter, and former staff members Stacy Overby and Rosanne Gueguen, were enthusiastic in their support of my project, while Lisa Kalmus, curator of the Corps Center, assisted with assembling the photographs. Dr. David Chapman, director of the Cushing Library and Archives, made researching the files in the university archives much easier.

Many people outside the university provided helpful and enthusiastic support to me. Dr. Henry Dethloff, author of *Texas Aggies Go to War*, was a mentor to my literary endeavor and always ready to provide much-appreciated advice. My late friend Calvin C. Boykin Jr. provided encouragement as well as access to his extensive files on Turney Leonard. His daughter, Anne Boykin, used her considerable talents to prepare the maps. April Serig, librarian at the Larry Ringer Public Library in College Station, was very helpful in locating many books for me through interlibrary loan. Steven Ruhnke, curator of the First Armored Division Museum, Baumholder, Germany, cleared up the mystery of Thomas Fowler's unit and also provided several photographs from the Italian campaign. And Denis Berger shared a rare copy of a booklet about the 191st Tank Battalion in World War II.

Special thanks are extended to Lt. Gen. John Van Alstyne (Ret.), commandant of the Corps of Cadets, and Donald "Buck" Henderson for their encouragement and support.

Carol Ann Honeycutt, my daughter, worked tirelessly in proofing each chapter and providing literary advice. My wife, Gloria, was unflagging in her support during the innumerable days and nights I spent at the word processor. She was always ready and willing to read and correct the rough drafts as they were produced.

Finally, the publisher, Texas A&M University Press, has been supportive in every conceivable way. My deepest gratitude goes to Charles Backus, Mary Lenn Dixon, Thom Lemmons, Diana Vance, Gayla Christiansen, Caitlin Churchill, and Kyle Littlefield.

TEXAS
AGGIE
MEDALS
OF
HONOR

THE SEARCH FOR THE
TEXAS AGGIE MEDALS
OF HONOR

Ask, and it shall be given you; seek, and ye shall find;
knock, and it shall open unto you.

MATTHEW 7:7

AS A FRESHMAN in the Corps of Cadets at the Agricultural and Mechanical College of Texas, I was required to learn the names of the Aggies awarded the Medal of Honor during World War II. At that time they were just names, I had no connection with them. I also had to know the names and jersey numbers of the football players as well as the names of each building on the campus and when it was built. There were many other facts about the campus and Texas A&M that had to be memorized, referred to as "campusology."

During that same year, I had my first connection with a Medal of Honor recipient. The first day of my freshman agronomy class, Eli L. Whiteley walked into the room and announced that he would be our instructor. Needless to say, the young cadets in the class were thrilled to have an instructor who had been awarded the Medal of Honor. It was not that long after the end of the war, and Whiteley still showed the scars of his grievous wounds. We wanted him to talk about the war, but he insisted that he would tell us about crops and soils.

Years later I discovered another connection upon learning that Turney W. Leonard's company commander in the 893rd Tank Destroyer Battalion was Marion Pugh, Class of 1941, the famous Aggie football player. Pugh grew up on the north side of Fort Worth, Texas, and graduated from North Side High School, my own alma mater. His parents and my maternal grandparents were longtime friends. I first met Pugh at an auction at his father's farm west of Lake Worth (a community west of Fort Worth) during the time his unit was training at the Tank Destroyer Center at Camp Hood, Texas. He was wearing his tanker coveralls with shiny lieutenant's bar and Tank Destroyer patch and was an impressive-looking soldier. In later years I visited with Pugh several times at his lumberyard in College Station, not knowing that he had fought with Leonard.

Several years ago I learned of a family connection with Horace S. Carswell. Like Pugh, he also grew up on the north side of Fort Worth and graduated from North Side High School. My aunt, Beverly Foster Potishman, attended high school with him and told me they had dated at one time.

Yet another connection was with Lloyd H. Hughes, who trained at Tarrant Field, Fort Worth, from November 1942 to January 1943. At the time I was living at Lake Worth, and my home was along the flight path for Tarrant Field. The B-24 bombers flew very low over my house when landing or taking off, and each time one came over, there was a loud roar that rattled the windows. This went on day and night during the war. If I was outside when a plane flew over, I would always wave. Sometimes there would be an airman standing in the waist gunners' door, and he would wave back. If I was on my horse in the pasture, I would try to race the bomber, but the bomber always won. In all probability Hughes flew over my house, and perhaps I raced him. At least I would like to think I waved at his plane.

The planning for the search required establishing a priority for locating family members. My initial efforts focused on William G. Harrell, who was the only marine of the seven, and George D. Keathley, who came from the earliest class of the group, while also gathering information on all of the recipients as time permitted. The search began at Internet locator sites, looking for people living in each recipient's hometown and with the same last name. These Web sites were of great value, though in several cases they listed invalid addresses. The *Directory of Former Students,* published by the Texas A&M Association of Former Students, was the principal source for finding Aggies with the same last name. Online research also extended to extensive searches of genealogy Web sites for family members and those of many World War II units for clues and contacts. This initial method was a shotgun approach to be sure, but it had proved effective earlier in searching for officers who had served in my battalion in Vietnam.

After a few weeks of planning, I took the first step by mailing letters to four people named Harrell in the San Antonio area. This was followed by several more letters to people named Harrell in the area where he had grown up. All together, sixteen letters went out: three were returned for insufficient address, and three people answered that they were not related. Internet research disclosed that Harrell had died in 1964 while employed at the Veteran's Administration Center in San Antonio and that he had four children, but their names remained unknown.

The first break in the search came when I located a Harrell family tree on the Internet, which led to contact with Lucy Brown of San Antonio. Her response to my e-mail request for information about the Harrell family stated that she had not known Harrell but that his daughter was her best friend in high school. Although the daughter was deceased, her mother, Larena Reidel, Harrell's first wife, lived in Fort Pierce, Florida. Brown thought that her friend's brother, William, lived in California. After finding Reidel's phone number online, my first call to Florida was answered by William Harrell, who confirmed that he was the son of William G. Harrell. He said that his mother had died recently and that he had moved from California, where he had been a parole officer and later an attorney, to care for her during her illness. When asked about his father's Medal of Honor, he said that he thought his half-brother, Gary, who lived in Punta Gorda, Florida, owned it. William had had no contact with him until recently but was able to provide a telephone number.

A phone call to Gary Harrell, a retired U.S. Navy commander who teaches a history course at Edison Community College, revealed that he had the medal (which he occasionally used in his class). When asked about displaying it in the Sanders Corps of Cadets Center, he said he was having dinner with his sister, Christy, who was visiting from Chicago, that night and would discuss it with her.

A letter to Gary Harrell dated December 11, 2007, included a picture of the bronze bas-relief plaque of his father in the Corps Center and another of the display case honoring Turney Leonard to give him an idea of how his father's medal would be displayed. A call to Gary a week later proved to be a disappointment. He said he wanted to keep the medal for use in his history course but would consider placing the samurai sword his father brought back from Iwo Jima in the Corps Center. The sword had played a part in the action in which Harrell was wounded and was mentioned in his Medal of Honor citation. But hope was not lost, for Gary was planning a trip to Houston the last week in January 2008 and wanted to visit the Corps Center at College Station.

On Saturday, January 26, Stacy Overby, director of the Corps Center, and Lisa Kalmus, the center curator, welcomed Gary and his wife. Following a tour of the center, which included viewing the dormitory named for his father, he promised to bring the samurai sword on his next visit to Texas. He also said that he would change his will and leave the medal to Texas A&M so that, at some time in the future, William G. Harrell's Medal of Honor will be displayed in the Corps Center.

Further online research revealed that Lloyd H. Hughes's medal was displayed in a museum in Refugio, Texas. My first inclination was to delay contacting the museum, since I doubted that it would give up a Medal of Honor awarded to a local man, and instead decided to contact the family.

On December 9, 2007, I came across a posting on Ancestry.com about Hughes, but I had to be a member to access the site and contact the poster. After deciding to subscribe to the site, I made contact with Rebecca Ann Jordan of Austin. She is a niece of Hughes and is interested in family genealogy, especially concerning her uncle. She had a Web site devoted to Hughes that provided a wealth of information about his life.

I introduced myself and told her of my project. Jordan related that as a young girl, she had attended the on-campus ceremony in 1969 when the dormitories were renamed for those Aggies awarded the Medal of Honor, recalling particularly the corps review and sitting behind a general during the parade. She said that the family called Hughes "Pete," and before long I was thinking of and referring to him by that name. She was confused about my quest because she thought that Texas A&M had all seven Medals of Honor displayed in the Memorial Student Center. This is a common misconception among students, former students, and visitors to the campus. I explained that the medals in the Memorial Student Center are reproductions and not the actual awards. I also told her about the authentic Leonard and Whiteley medals displayed in the Corps Center.

She was not sure if the medal in Refugio was loaned or donated to the museum and suggested that I talk to another uncle, John Jordan, who lived in Corpus Christi. I called him on November 11, and during a long conversation he said that he was under the impression the medal had been loaned to the museum. I explained my project and how we really wanted the medal for display at Texas A&M. Jordan seemed receptive to the idea since many family members were Aggies and he had a grandson then at the university. He said there was a family reunion scheduled for December 29 in Corpus Christi and that he would discuss the matter with other family members then. The next day I mailed him pictures of the Hughes plaque in the Corps Center and the Turney Leonard display as well as a Corps Center brochure. Three days later Jordan called with a question about the medals in the Memorial Student Center. Once again I explained that they were reproductions.

While this was going on, information surfaced that some military medals had been stolen from the Refugio museum. A longtime collector of such items, I was aware of the value of an original Medal of Honor, especially a well-documented medal awarded for the Ploesti raid. Even though it is illegal to buy or sell a Medal of Honor, it is also illegal to steal one. On the black market, the Hughes medal would be worth several thousand dollars and probably would be sold overseas. In conversations with the Jordans, I emphasized that the Corps Center contained a gun collection worth several million dollars and many other valuable items, so security had the highest priority.

On December 17 I met with Lt. Gen. John Van Alstyne, commandant of cadets, to inform him of my project. This was the first time any university official knew of my search for the Aggie Medals of Honor. I requested that someone contact John Jordan to request the Hughes medal be displayed in the Corps Center. The following day General Van Alstyne sent a letter to Jordan requesting that the medal be displayed in the center.

About two weeks later I called Jordan, who gave me the good news that the family had agreed that the proper place for the Hughes medal was at Texas A&M. Jordan's son, John Paul, was charged to retrieve the medal from the Refugio museum and deliver it to the Corps Center. On April 11, 2008, I met with him at the Hilton Hotel in College Station, and he entrusted the medal to me. John Paul also had with him the service medals that Hughes had earned, along with documents, books, and pictures. The following Monday the medals were delivered to the Corps Center and the books given to the center library; the documents and pictures have been placed in the university archives with the completion of this book.

During the process of gathering items for the Hughes display, Rebecca Jordan introduced me by e-mail to Sharon Ewing, a niece of Hughes's wife, Hazel. Ewing said that she had a Bank of England ten-shilling note Hughes had sent to his wife after his unit arrived in the British Isles. The shilling note contained the signatures of Hughes, the three other officers of his B-24 crew, twenty-eight officers of the squadron, and that of Capt. Philip Ardery, squadron commander of the 564th Bomb Squadron, along with the notation "To my wife Hazel." Ewing agreed to place the note in the Hughes display.

While working on securing the Hughes medal, I began writing to everyone named Keathley living in Olney, Texas, sending four letters on November 11, 2007, to Keathleys listed in the *Directory of Former Students*. A few days later Marlin Keathley called from Oklahoma City, Oklahoma. He said that he had received my letter, was George Keathley's younger brother, and had information on the location of the medal. Keathley explained that the medal had hung on his wall until a few years earlier, when he gave it to his cousin, Carla Perry, of Olney. Perry had requested it for display at the dedication of the Young County War Memorial in Graham, Texas, after which she placed it in the local museum. Keathley also mentioned the controversy concerning placing his brother's name on the war memorial, an interesting item that begged for further investigation. Now three of the five medals had apparently been located. But once again, the specter of retrieving one from a local museum rose in my path.

I took the information about the location of Keathley's medal to General Van Alystne, asking that Carla Perry be contacted. His office sent a letter on December 12, 2007, requesting that the medal be loaned to Texas A&M for display in the Corps Center. While awaiting a reply, I wanted to confirm that the medal was actually on display in the museum in Graham. Research revealed that the county agent was an Aggie who thus seemed to be a good, confidential source to do some detective work in town. A call to the county agent's office was answered by Michelle McClanahan, who said the county agent, James "Brad" Morrison, was out of the office. When asked about the medal, she did not remember seeing it in the museum and thought it might be on display in the county courthouse. I asked her to check both places for the medal.

On January 7, 2008, Morrison called back and said the medal was not in Graham and that I should talk to Dorman Holub, pastor of Eastside Church of Christ in Graham and who was active in the local historical society. Holub said he knew Carla Perry and would talk to her about the medal and also provided the names and location of the Keathley daughters. Later that same day he called to say that Perry only had the medal for a few days during the memorial dedication and had returned it to Paula Roy, Keathley's daughter, of Wichita Falls. Perry told him that Marlin Keathley was confused about the medal, which had been in the possession of George Keathley's wife, Inez, until her death and since then had been with Roy.

The commandant's office received a letter from Perry on January 10 that confirmed the medal was held by Paula Roy. I called Roy that same day and spoke with her husband, Philip. He said that they had contacted someone at the Texas A&M University Archives several years ago about placing the medal there. He also provided valuable information about the Keathley family. Immediately afterward I contacted David Chapman, Texas A&M University archivist, who was not aware of any discussions with the university about the medal. Later that same day I spoke with Paula Roy, who said that she would talk with her sister Helen, who lives in San Angelo, about displaying the medal at Texas A&M.

Afterward I asked the director of the Corps Center to send Paula Roy a letter requesting that the medal be loaned to Texas A&M for display. On January 19 a call to Roy confirmed that the family had agreed to the request, and we made arrangements for me to pick up the medal in Wichita Falls. On January 23 I made the long drive, accompanied by my friend Lt. Col. Donald R. "Buck" Henderson (ret.), Class of 1962. While visiting with the Roys, they showed us a scrapbook containing newspaper articles about Keathley and several of his letters written from Italy, several of which they kindly photocopied. Henderson and I returned late that night to College Station, the next morning delivering the medal to Stacy Overby at the Corps Center.

The search for the Fowler medal began with mailing letters to people named Fowler in the Wichita Falls area, later expanded to Dallas after research online suggested that his son might live there. I wrote to several Thomas Fowlers in the Dallas area but received no replies. Since Fowler's Medal of Honor citation listed his unit as the 1st Armored Division, I researched Web sites for that division but found no mention of Fowler. This was suspicious since divisional sites invariably mention their Medal of Honor recipients. Further research identified the three tank battalions organic to the division during World War II, but sites dedicated to those battalions again made no mention of Fowler.

The next step was to contact the 1st Armored Division Museum in Germany to see if they had any information. An e-mail message was immediately answered by Steven Ruhnke, the museum's curator, who stated that the medal citation mistakenly lists Fowler as a member of the 1st Armored Division when in fact he was assigned to the 191st Tank Battalion, a separate unit serving with the Fifth Army. This dilemma solved, I soon found an address for the 191st Tank Battalion Association and sent a letter to Denis Berger, the reunion coordinator of the association. He called me a few days later, providing information about the battalion and offering to send me a booklet entitled *191st Tank Battalion,* which was published in Germany at the end of the war. This history of the battalion proved to be a valuable source for writing an account of the battalion's wartime activities. Berger also sent a staff study written at the Armor School in 1948 by a former member of the battalion, a battalion shoulder patch, and a set of battalion crests. He suggested that I call Fowler's platoon sergeant, Oscar L. Smith, of Jacksonville, Texas. Smith was with Fowler at the time of his death and related the events of his final hours.

But the clue that led to finding Fowler's son (and his medal) came from Rebecca Ann Jordan, Hughes's niece. She suggested that I contact the Museum of North Texas History in Wichita Falls since they had a display for Fowler. An e-mail to the staff was answered by Mary Kearby, a volunteer with the Wichita County Archives, who provided information about Fowler, including a crucial fact that Fowler's widow had remarried in Denver, Colorado, to Erlon E. Nowell. The search now shifted to Colorado, and a locator search revealed an address for a Thomas W. Fowler Jr. in Denver. His response to my letter confirmed that he was Fowler's son and that he had his father's Medal of Honor.

The fifth medal belonged to Horace S. Carswell and proved to be the most difficult to locate. Internet research revealed that Dr. J'Nell Pate, an author and retired history professor from Fort Worth, had written an article about Carswell that appeared in the *West Texas Historical Association Yearbook* several years earlier. I sent her an e-mail and received a prompt reply stating that she would send me a copy of her article and that she believed Carswell's son, Robert Ede Carswell, was in Florida. A locater search listed a Robert Ede Carswell living in Indiantown, Florida. Although his birthday and wife's name matched the information I had for Carswell's son, two letters to the Florida address were not answered or returned and many phone calls went unreturned. A third letter was sent by certified mail, return receipt requested. The receipt was returned and contained the initials "REC" in the signature blank. I could only conclude that he did not want to communicate.

I decided that if I could not contact the son, then I would go to Fort Worth to conduct some additional research on Carswell. I had read that his portrait was hanging in the Fort Worth City Hall and that there was a monument, dedicated in 1995, at the former Carswell Air Force Base, now the Naval Air Station Joint Reserve Base. I went to City Hall, but no one knew about a portrait of Carswell. And at the headquarters of the naval air station, no one could be found who knew about the monument. I then went to the headquarters of the Texas Air National Guard unit on the same base. Again no one had ever heard of a monument until I started talking to an officer who happened to walk up to the information desk. His name was Lt. Col. Trevor Noel, Class of 1981, a cadet at Texas A&M when I was commandant of cadets. He said that he had attended the dedication of the Carswell monument and that it was located in front of the navy headquarters. After I told him it was no longer there, he replied that if it was on the base, he would find it. I contacted J'Nell Pate about the missing portrait and monument; she replied that she would contact some local historians about it. Later she e-mailed that she had been told that the monument was in an area behind the operations building but was not accessible to the public. I passed this information to Noel, who said he would check it out. He called two weeks later to report that the monument could not be located and that no one at the base seemed to know what had happened to it.

In September 2008 I sent an e-mail to the *Fort Worth Star-Telegram* suggesting that they investigate the situation with the monument and portrait since it appeared that Fort Worth had forsaken its World War II hero. A prompt reply stated that a reporter would be assigned to investigate the matter. Two months later a *Star-Telegram* reporter called to say that he had been assigned the story. He called again a few days later to report that the monument had been located at the base airfield near the control tower and that the portrait was on display in the city hall of White Settlement, a suburb of Fort Worth located adjacent to the Joint Reserve Base.

While in Fort Worth, I had visited the library at Texas Christian University to look at the yearbooks for the years Carswell was a student. Later I contacted the university and inquired about any on-campus memorials to Carswell, learning that there were none.

On March 30, 2009, a ceremony was held in the Sanders Corps of Cadets Center to honor 2nd Lt. Lloyd H. Hughes. Twenty members of his family and four relatives of his wife, Hazel, attended. Also in the crowd of about one hundred people were two veterans of the Ploesti Raid and two other veterans who, though they did not fly the mission, were in North Africa with Hughes's bomb group. During the ceremony, two of Hughes's brothers, John Jordan and William Jordan, and a sister-in-law, Ann Jordan, presented his Medal of Honor to Texas A&M. It is now on display in the center.

Another ceremony, on July 17, 2009, was held in the Corps Center to honor SSgt. George D. Keathley. Twenty-one members of the Keathley family attended. About one hundred guests were in the audience to watch his daughters, Helen Haggard and Paula Roy, along with a nephew, Len Keathley, present his Medal of Honor to Texas A&M. It too is on display in the center.

On November 6, 2009, the Thomas W. Fowler medal was placed in the Corps Center. The display includes photos, cadet insignia, 191st Tank Battalion patch, unit crests, Purple Heart, and campaign medals.

On May 29, 2010, before a large crowd in the Corps Center, the Harrell family presented their father's Medal of Honor to Texas A&M. They also presented a Samurai sword, Purple Heart, and other medals for display.

HISTORY OF THE MEDAL OF HONOR

ABOVE AND BEYOND THE CALL OF DUTY

THE MEDAL OF HONOR is the highest military award that can be given to any individual by the United States of America. Conceived in the early 1860s, the medal has a colorful and inspiring history that has culminated in the standards applied today for awarding this respected decoration.

In their provisions for judging potential recipients, each of the armed services has established regulations that permit no margin of doubt or error. The deed of the person must be proven by incontestable evidence of at least two eyewitnesses; it must be so outstanding that it clearly distinguishes one's gallantry beyond the call of duty from other forms of bravery; it must involve risk of life; and it must be the type of deed that, if the nominee had not done it, would not result in any justified rebuke.

Apart from the great tribute it conveys, there are certain privileges that accompany the Medal of Honor. Its recipients can, under certain conditions, obtain free military air transportation. Special identification cards and military commissary and exchange privileges are provided for them and their qualified dependents. Children of recipients are eligible for admission to any of the military academies. Finally, recipients can receive a special pension of more than $1,000 per month.

The Medal of Honor is presented to its recipients by a high official "in the name of the Congress of the United States"; for this reason it is sometimes called the Congressional Medal of Honor. As a general rule, the Medal of Honor may be awarded for a deed of personal bravery or self-sacrifice above and beyond the call of duty only while the person is a member of the U.S. armed forces in action against an enemy of the United States, while engaged in military operations involving conflict with a hostile foreign force, or while serving with friendly foreign forces engaged against an opposing armed force in an armed conflict to which the United States is not a belligerent party. But until passage of Public Law 88–77, the navy could and did award Medals of Honor for bravery in the line of the naval profession, whether in times of peace or war. Such awards recognized bravery in saving life and other deeds of valor performed in submarine rescues, boiler explosions, turret fires, or other types of uniquely naval disasters.

The Medal of Honor was not the idea of any one person. Like most concepts that have flowered into institutions and practices in our country, it was the result of group thought and action and evolved in response to a need of the times.

In the winter of 1861–62, following the outbreak of the Civil War, there was much thought in Washington concerning the necessity for recognizing the deeds of the Federal soldiers, sailors, and marines who were distinguishing themselves in the fighting. In 1861 Sen. James W. Grimes of Iowa introduced a bill to create a navy medal. Congress passed the measure and Pres. Abraham Lincoln signed it on December 21, 1861, thus establishing a Medal of Honor for enlisted men of the navy and Marine Corps. This was the first decoration formally authorized by the U.S. government to be worn as a badge of honor. Action on an army medal was started two months later, when on February 17, 1862, Sen. Henry Wilson of Massachusetts introduced a Senate resolution providing for presentation of "medals of honor" to enlisted men of the army and volunteer forces who "shall most distinguish themselves by their gallantry in action, and other soldier like qualities." President Lincoln's signature on July 12 made the resolution law. It was amended by an act approved on March 3, 1863, that extended its provision to include officers as well as enlisted men and made the provisions retroactive to the beginning of the Civil War. This legislation was to stand as the basis upon which the Army Medal of Honor could be awarded until July 9, 1918, when it was superseded by a completely revised statute.

After the approval of the navy medal, Secretary of the Navy Gideon Welles wrote to James Pollack, director of the U.S. Mint at Philadelphia, asking for his assistance in obtaining a design. Pollock had submitted five proposals to the navy by the time the army bill had been introduced in the Senate. When he learned of the army bill, Pollack wrote to Secretary of War Edwin M. Stanton, enclosing one of the designs prepared for the navy and pointing out that it would be appropriate for use by the army as well. Two more designs were submitted before the navy approved one on May 9, 1862.

The medal adopted was an inverted five-pointed star two inches long suspended from an anchor and attached to a red, white, and blue ribbon. Pollock explained that one of the two figures at the center of the star on the obverse side represented the foul spirit of secession and rebellion. The crouching male figure holds in his hands serpents with forked tongues striking at a large female figure representing the Union, or "Genius of our Country." Based on Minerva, the Roman goddess of wisdom and the arts, she is wearing a helmet bearing an eagle while holding in her right hand a shield and in her left the fasces. Around these figures are thirty-four stars representing the states in the Union at that time. In later years this engraving came to be known as "Minerva Repulsing Discord."

On November 17, 1862, the War Department contracted with the firm William Wilson and Sons, Philadelphia, where the navy medals were being made, for 2,000 of the same type for the army. Stanton wanted a distinctive design for the army, so the anchor was replaced by a spread-winged eagle standing on crossed cannons and cannonballs. At each wingtip the eagle was attached to the ribbon, which like its naval counterpoint utilized the national colors. The reverse of the medal was left blank except for the words "Personal Valor." [1]

During the Civil War, 1,522 Medals of Honor were awarded: 1,198 to soldiers, 307 to sailors, and seventeen to marines. The first act so honored occurred on February 13, 1861, when Asst. Surgeon Bernard J. D. Irwin took command of troops and attacked and defeated hostile Indians on his way to rescuing sixty-one soldiers of the 7th Infantry trapped by Chiricahua Apaches at Apache Pass, Arizona Territory. Although the medal had not yet been proposed in Congress, the award was approved after adoption and was presented to Irwin in 1894. On May 24, 1861, in Alexandria, Virginia, Pvt. Francis Edwin Brownell performed the first action of the Civil War to merit the Medal of Honor. Brownell was a member of the 11th New York Infantry, and in the first days of the war, as his unit entered Alexandria, a Confederate flag was spotted atop an inn. Col. E. E. Ellsworth led a group into the inn and tore down the flag. As the Federals descended the stairs, the innkeeper killed Ellsworth with a shotgun blast to the chest. Brownell responded by fatally shooting the innkeeper. His citation reads, "Killed the murderer of Colonel Ellsworth at the Marshall House, Alexandria. Virginia."

Another medal was awarded to Dr. Mary Walker, one of the first woman physicians in the country and the only female to receive the Medal of Honor. At the outbreak of war, Dr. Walker applied for a commission as an army surgeon but was turned down because of her gender. She served as a volunteer field surgeon during the war and was taken prisoner while serving as assistant surgeon with the 52nd Ohio Infantry. After four months in a Richmond prison, she was exchanged for a Confederate officer. Following the war, she lobbied for a brevet promotion to major for her services but was turned down because she was never an officer. Pres. Andrew Johnson asked Secretary of War Stanton if there was some way to recognize her service, to which Stanton ordered a Medal of Honor prepared for Walker. It was presented to her in January 1866, and she wore it every day for the rest of her life. In 1916, when the standards were revised to include actions only in "actual combat with an enemy," her medal was rescinded, but she refused to return it and continued to wear it even after being told this was illegal.

In 1863 Lincoln authorized Medals of Honor to any member of the 27th Maine Volunteer Infantry who reenlisted for another tour of duty. Of the 864 members of the regiment, 309 men remained, and the rest going home. Through a clerical error, not only did the 309 volunteers receive the medal but also those who had gone home despite the president's offer.

Valorous acts during the Indian Wars resulted in 426 awards of the Medal of Honor. Five civilian scouts, including William F. "Buffalo Bill" Cody, were so decorated. Twenty-four medals were awarded for action in the Battle of the Little Big Horn, "Custer's Last Stand." Sgt. Richard Hanley, of Lt. Col. George Armstrong Custer's 7th Cavalry Regiment, was one of those men. Hanley rode directly into the enemy's line of fire to recover a mule laden with much needed ammunition. His officers shouted for him to give up the effort, but he remained exposed to a rain of arrows and bullets for twenty minutes until he captured the mule. Another 7th Cavalry soldier, Sgt. Benjamin Criswell, was awarded the medal for riding to the rescue of the wounded Lt. Benjamin Hodgson, whose horse was down. With Indians firing furiously and closing in on him, Criswell wheeled his horse around Hodgson and waited for the wounded man to grab the stirrup. He then galloped away, dragging Hodgson across the river to the opposite side. As they reached the bank, though, the officer was shot in the head and killed. Criswell dismounted under fire and threw the lieutenant's body over his horse, then moved among the dead horses on the riverbank and picked up saddlebags full of ammunition before returning to his lines. Also killed at the Little Big Horn was the colonel's brother, Tom Custer, who had received two Medals of Honor for capturing Confederate flags during the Civil War.[2]

In 1896 the army changed the ribbon on its medal. In 1904, as a result of widespread imitation by veterans groups, most notably the Grand Army of the Republic, the army adopted a new design. Conceived by Brig. Gen. George Gillespie, a Civil War recipient, the new army medal was a five-pointed star with a profile of Minerva at the center, surrounded by a green enameled laurel wreath. The army eagle now rested on a bar reading "VALOR." Supporting the medal was a blue silk ribbon spangled with thirteen stars. Gillespie received a patent for his design, which he turned over to the secretary of war and his successors. After the patent expired in 1918, Congress passed a law forbidding the unauthorized duplication of military medals.

The Army Reorganization Act of June 3, 1916, provided for the appointment by the secretary of war of a board of retired general officers for the purpose of "investigating and reporting upon past awards or issue of the so-called congressional medal of honor by or through the War Department; this with a view to ascertain what Medals of Honor, if any, have been awarded or issued for any cause other than distinguished conduct involving actual conflict with an enemy."

The board met on October 16, gathered all Medal of Honor records, prepared statistics, classified cases, and organized evidence that might be needed in its deliberations. By January 17, 1917, all of the 2,625 Medals of Honor awarded up to that time were considered by the board, and on February 15 the names of 911 individuals were stricken from the list. Of these 911 names, 864 were from one group, the 27th Maine Volunteer Infantry. Among those who lost their medal were William F. "Buffalo Bill" Cody, Dr. Mary Walker, and members of Lincoln's funeral escort. There have been no instances of cancellation of Medal of Honor awards within the naval service.[3]

In 1919 the navy, which had awarded scores of Medals of Honor for peacetime bravery, created a different design to recognize actual combat action. A Maltese cross, designed by Tiffany and Company of New York (and known as the Tiffany Cross), bore the American eagle surrounded by four anchors. It was attached to a red-starred ribbon with a bar that inexplicably bore the British spelling "VALOUR." Only a handful of men, mostly during World War I, received this style of medal. Noncombat acts of valor continued to be recognized with the star design of the Medal of Honor, now with a ribbon similar to the army model. In 1942 Congress eliminated the Tiffany Cross, and once again all naval personnel were eligible for only one Medal of Honor design, the original star.[4]

Minor wars and campaigns accounted for additional awards. One hundred and ten medals were awarded during the Spanish American War. During the Philippine Insurrection (1899–1902), eighty were awarded for actions above and beyond the call of duty. The Boxer Rebellion (1900) in China accounted for the award of fifty-nine medals. Forty-six of the fifty-six medals awarded during the Veracruz campaign (1914) went to naval personnel; one was awarded to a soldier and nine to marines.

The United States entered World War I in April 1917, and by November 11, 1918 (Armistice Day), 124 Medals of Honor had been awarded. One of the best-known recipients was Sgt. Alvin York, who single-handedly killed twenty-four Germans, silenced thirty-five machine guns, and took 132 prisoners. Another man who became a household name was Capt. Eddie Rickenbacker, the "ace of aces." Rickenbacker downed twenty-eight enemy planes in only five months of combat.

In all, 464 Medals of Honor were awarded during World War II. Fifteen men received the decoration for their heroic actions at Pearl Harbor on December 7, 1941. Only five of those men survived their moment of heroism, one of them dying in action eleven months later. Gen. Douglas MacArthur was awarded the medal in Australia after being evacuated from the Philippines. His award is one of the few of the war that could be described as "symbolic," in large part because the general's Philippine Army was an inspiration to the American people during those dark days. Interestingly, his father, Maj. Gen. Arthur MacArthur, earned a Medal of Honor for rallying Union troops on November 25, 1863, at Missionary Ridge, Tennessee, during the Civil War.

The first five months of the war were unremittingly bleak. That was to change in April 1942, when Lt. Col. Jimmy Doolittle led a carrier-based force of B-25 bombers on a daring raid over Japan. The operation was a great psychological blow to the enemy and raised the spirit of Americans—the first piece of good news in the war. When Doolittle learned from Gen. George C. Marshall that he was to receive the Medal of Honor, the colonel protested that he did not deserve it. Marshall said gravely and quietly, "I think you do." Doolittle later led the Eighth Air Force in the European theater.[5]

One of the first marine casualties during the landings on Iwo Jima on February 19, 1945, was Sgt. John Basilone. He had received one of the Marine Corps' first Medals of Honor of World War II after leading the defense that held off a night-long *banzai* charge on Guadalcanal in 1942. After a much-publicized return to the United States, the veteran volunteered to return to combat just in time for Iwo Jima. Twenty-seven medals were awarded for the Iwo Jima campaign, twenty-two to marines and five to navy corpsmen.[6]

America's next war was in Korea. Just before dawn on June 25, 1950, the North Korean People's Army swept across the border into South Korea. They met little organized resistance and three days later captured Seoul, the capital of South Korea. By that time the South Korean army had lost three-quarters of its original men. On June 26 Pres. Harry Truman dispatched the U.S. Navy and Air Force to the South Koreans' aid. The next night, one hour after the fall of Seoul, the United Nations Security Council passed a resolution calling on all members to help South Korea repel the attack. On June 30 Truman granted General MacArthur's request for U.S. ground forces to stop the Communist tide. The first troops were rushed in from occupation duty in Japan and were soon followed by elements of the small post–World War II regular army. Before the war ended, 5.5 million Americans would serve in Korea. Ultimately, twenty-one nations contributed troops or other direct assistance to the South Koreans.

During the conflict, Truman sought neither a declaration of war nor the informal approval of Congress. "Police action" was the term the White House preferred to described the fighting. What many believed would be a short war lasted three years, to be concluded only by an armistice on July 27, 1953. One hundred thirty three Medals of Honor were awarded during the Korean Conflict: eighty to soldiers, seven to sailors, forty-two to marines, and four to airmen. Ninety-five medals were conferred posthumously.[7]

Maj. Gen. William F. Dean, commanding general, 24th Infantry Division, stationed in Japan, led the first combat troops into Korea. His division was committed piecemeal as a delaying force while U.N. forces organized a counter-attack. Dean was captured and spent three years as a prisoner of war. He was awarded the Medal of Honor for his personal bravery in the front lines.

Pfc. Herbert K Pililaau of Hawaii was serving with the 23rd Infantry Regiment on Heartbreak Ridge when he volunteered to cover the withdrawal of his company. Armed with a Browning automatic rifle, Pililaau remained on top of the hill, firing his weapon at the onrushing enemy until he exhausted his ammunition, then hit them with grenades. When his grenades were used up, he pulled out his trench knife and fought on. After he was wounded, Pililaau fell to the ground and was bayoneted by the attackers.[8]

America soon became involved in a different kind of war in Southeast Asia. Beginning in 1950 with a small force of military "advisors" in French Indochina, U.S. military personnel did no real advising until the French departed in 1956. By 1964 the number of advisers had grown to 10,000 men. Steady escalation of the fighting there led to a force of more than 500,000 Americans serving in Vietnam by 1968. Several other countries provided forces to support the South Vietnamese, most notably South Korea, Thailand, Australia, and New Zealand.

The first person awarded the Medal of Honor in the Vietnam War was Capt. Roger H. C. Donlon. He commanded a twelve-man Special Forces team and a force of three hundred men, mostly South Vietnamese and Montagnards, defending an outpost in the central highlands. On the night of July 5, 1964, his outpost was attacked by a force of Vietcong, estimated at more than eight hundred strong. Donlon was wounded several times during the night and, despite his injuries, moved through the camp, firing at the enemy, treating the wounded, shouting encouragement, and directing the defenders' fire. Donlon's force fought through the night, and by daylight, the enemy had retreated, leaving behind more than fifty dead. The captain was evacuated and spent several months in the hospital. After recovering from his wounds, he attended a White House ceremony to receive his Medal of Honor.[9]

One of the thirteen medals awarded to air force personnel during the Vietnam War went to Lt. Col. Joe M. Jackson, a Korean War veteran and former U-2 pilot. During the evacuation of the Special Forces camp at Kham Duc in the central highlands, three men were left behind. After one unsuccessful rescue attempt by a C-123 transport plane, the airborne commander asked for a volunteer to go in for another try. Flying another C-123 in the vicinity, Jackson realized that he was in the best position to land. Landing under heavy enemy fire, Jackson spotted the three men in a ditch, but debris prevented him from taxiing any closer to them. As the C-123 turned to take off the way it came in, the three jumped from the culvert and ran for the plane under fire from positions farther down the runway. Reaching the aircraft, they jumped into the open cargo door at the rear. Jackson taxied around an unexploded shell on the runway, applied full power, and took off under heavy fire from the hills on either side. The plane had been on the ground at Kham Duc for less than a minute. Eight months later Pres. Lyndon Johnson placed the air force Medal of Honor around Jackson's neck.[10]

In both world wars, U.S. Army Air Corps pilots received the army Medal of Honor. Even in Korea, after the U.S. Air Force had become a separate service, its men continued to receive the army design. In 1963 the air force created its own medal, first presented to Vietnam flyers. The air force Medal of Honor is similar to the army medal, with the head of the Statue of Liberty replacing Minerva and an air force blue ribbon attachment more specific to that service.[11]

With U.S. involvement in subsequent, current, and future military actions, the medal will continue to be awarded. Two Special Forces soldiers, M.Sgt. Gary I. Gordon and Sfc. Randall D. Shughart, were awarded posthumous medals for actions in the 1993 "Black Hawk Down" incident in Somalia. As of 2009, one medal has been awarded to a navy SEAL in Afghanistan and four have been awarded in Iraq.

The sanctity of the Medal of Honor continues to be of interest to the military services, Congress, and the Congressional Medal of Honor Society.

In June 1977 Army Secretary Clifford Alexander Jr. ordered the restoration of the Civil War award of the Medal of Honor to Dr. Mary Walker. In June 1989 the U.S. Army restored the Medals of Honor to five civilian scouts from the Indian Wars, including "Buffalo Bill" Cody. World War I had yielded no African American Medal of Honor recipients, not due to any lack of courage by America's "soldiers of color" but to the unjust prejudices of the time. On April 24, 1991, Pres. George H. W. Bush corrected this omission when he presented the medal to the family of Cpl. Freddie Stowers, an African American who had died in his moment of valor in France in 1918.[12]

After a comprehensive review of military awards to World War II black soldiers, on January 20, 1998, Pres. Bill Clinton presented Medals of Honor to the families of six deceased black servicemen and one to a surviving veteran, Vernon Baker.[13]

On June 21, 2000, Clinton presented the medal to twenty-two other World War II veterans, many posthumously. All went to Asian Americans who had been denied earlier recognition due to racism. Among the recipients was Sen. Daniel K. Inouye of Hawaii. Twenty of the twenty-two were members of either the 100th Infantry Battalion or the 442nd Regimental Combat Team, both of which were all-volunteer units and among the most decorated units in U.S. military history.[14]

In ceremonies at the White House on January 16, 2001, President Clinton presented a posthumous Medal of Honor to Theodore Roosevelt, who had been denied the medal after the Spanish American War. This disapproval is widely believed to have been the result of political pressure. Roosevelt's son, Brig. Gen. Theodore Roosevelt Jr., had been awarded the medal in World War II for his actions during the D-Day invasion. This award provided a second instance of father and son recipients of the medal, the first being the MacArthurs.[15]

On Armistice Day, 1921, a Medal of Honor was pinned on the flag draping the coffin of the Unknown Soldier at Arlington National Cemetery by Pres. Warren G. Harding. At the same time the president pinned on the flag the highest awards of Great Britain, France, Belgium, Italy, Romania, Poland, and Czechoslovakia.[16]

During the interwar period, special congressional action and executive orders allowed the award of the Medal of Honor to the unknown soldiers of Great Britain, France, Italy, Belgium, and Romania. The medal was also awarded to the Unknown Soldier of World War II, the Korean Conflict, and the Vietnam War.[17]

A total of 3,467 Medals of Honor have been awarded to members of the U.S. armed forces, including the five medals to foreign "unknowns." Over 60 percent of the Medals of Honor awarded during World War II, Korea, Vietnam, Somalia, Afghanistan, and Iraq have been conferred posthumously. Recipients who survived their valorous actions, though, have found their lives forever changed. One day they are ordinary soldiers, anonymous as any in the armed forces, and the next they are declared the bravest of the brave. Their picture appears in newspapers and their families become subject to publicity. Then there are the hometown parades, the public speeches, the talks to veteran groups, and the autographs.

Even years after the associated war has ended, the medal is a powerful force in the recipient's life. It is uncommon for one to use the medal for personal gain. Most modern recipients speak modestly of it and are reluctant to make a special case of themselves; instead, most strive to uphold its dignity. It is, in the words of Ronald Ray, a Vietnam recipient, an "awesome responsibility."[18]

LLOYD HERBERT HUGHES JR.
CLASS OF 1943

"Why do men do such things?"

CAPT. PHILIP P. ARDERY, COMMANDING OFFICER,

564TH BOMB SQUADRON

THE STORY OF Lloyd Herbert Hughes Jr. began in Alexandria, Louisiana, on July 12, 1921. The son of Lloyd Herbert Hughes Sr. and Mildred Mae Rainey Hughes, his family and friends called him "Pete." Apparently his parents divorced after his birth, and little is known about his father or the son's early years. In November 1923 Mildred began working as the postmaster of the Onalaska Post Office in Polk County, Texas. She married John Raymond Jordan in 1924 and continued to work as postmaster until February 1, 1925. In 1927 the Jordan family was living in Oak Hurst, San Jacinto County, Texas, but in 1929 they had moved to Huntsville, Texas. During this period three sons, James Marion, John Raymond Jr., and William Curtis, were added to the family. By 1930 John Jordan was a laborer working for the railroad in Trinity County, and the family lived in Josserand, Texas. Another son, Paul Nelson, was born in 1931. Thereafter the family made the long trip from Josserand to Refugio, Texas, packed in an old, canvas-topped Ford Model T.

Lloyd Hughes started school in Oakhurst, Texas, in 1927 but spent most of his school years in the Refugio school system. At the seventh-grade graduation, he was valedictorian of his class and received the American Legion award. In the eighth grade he was on the tennis team, the following year also participating in football while lettering in track, tennis, and basketball. In the tenth grade he was elected captain of the basketball squad. By his senior year Hughes was captain of the football team, received all-district mention, and was president of the boy's glee club. Like many students in the 1930s, he worked after school and during the summers, including an ice route and a newspaper route, being an usher at the local movie theater, and working summers as a roughneck in the oil fields during high school.[1]

An article appearing in the *Refugio County Press* in 2007 captures the essence of Hughes's boyhood:

> The home on Plasuela Street where 2d Lt. Lloyd Herbert "Pete" Hughes grew up is gone. Telltale signs that a house might have stood there are the thick growth of hackberry and anaqua trees that flank two sides of the property and a crowded row of giant salt cedars across the back.
>
> On Memorial Day, a wind from a nearby raincloud rustled through the thick salt cedars, releasing sounds similar to faint squeals from children at play.
>
> On this spot more than 60 years ago, a band of brothers, bonded by friendship, aroused the best of the spirit of America.
>
> Pete and his friends Benny Jones, Will and John Borglund, Dick Bartow,

[and] Rex Pitzer and Pete's three brothers, James, John, and Paul Jordan gathered regularly on this now-abandoned lot for games of football, baseball, monopoly, or just fooling around.

A member of the Refugio High School Class of 1939, Pete was the kind of guy who looked out for his friends and their little brothers. A Bobcat offensive end, Pete was tall, strong, and respected. "If there was a bully picking on you, Pete would straighten that out." John Borglund says.

The old water tower across the street challenged at least two of the athletes. For fun, Benny and Pete often kicked the football as high as they could muster in hope of hitting the water tower.

But that never happened.

The boys often met at the bubbles, a swimming hole near Lions/Shelly Park where a series of artesian wells once sent cool, fresh water foaming up into the Mission River. "Pete taught me how to swim at the bubbles," John said. "He was a big, strong kid. Benny was smaller, but he was strong for his size. When I tried to tackle him when we played football, it never fazed him, even when I hit him with all I had. Pete, Benny, and Will were real good friends."

Their halcyon days of football and youth ended abruptly on Dec. 7, 1941, the day bombs rained down on Pearl Harbor. The boys from the class of 1939 enlisted in droves.

Pete, who was at Texas A&M, joined the Army Air Corps and became a pilot. So did Benny and Rex. Fearless of heights, Dick became a paratrooper. His choice was not a surprise to the boys because Dick often climbed the railroad trestle bridge across the Mission River for fun while most of the fellows watched nervously. Will joined the Marines. The younger brothers of the band anxiously waited for their birthdays and their turn to serve.

Second Lt. Hughes was 21 when his wings were pinned on his uniform. A year later, he was flying in North Africa on the last mission of his life. Many others in the little band of Plasuela Street heroes also gave the ultimate sacrifice. The feisty member of the group, Benny, was commended for shooting down two German planes before he met his death in his cockpit.

Rex and his P-38 were shot down and lost as well. Will made it home alive but not unscathed. He received a Purple Heart for heroic service in the South Pacific. Dick was killed over Italy as he parachuted to the ground.

The little band of Refugio brothers all served their country, and all were decorated. During World War II, the U.S. became the most powerful force in the world. But victory is not found in equipment, skill, and weaponry alone. The American spirit, born with George Washington at Valley Forge, continues to manifest itself in communities like Refugio County, producing heroes like Pete Hughes and his band of brothers, who once kicked footballs at the town's water tower.[2]

In early 1939 the Jordan family moved to Corpus Christi, but Hughes remained in Refugio to complete school. Graduating from Refugio High School that spring, the six-foot-two-inch, 184-pound young man was interested in a career in the oil industry. Enrolling in Texas A&M in the fall of 1939, he elected petroleum engineering as his major. As a freshman in the Corps of Cadets, he was assigned to Company G, Infantry.

His academic record the first semester was less than stellar, and Hughes withdrew from school at the end of the first semester. Returning to Corpus Christi, he enrolled at Corpus Christi Junior College (later Del Mar College) and attended two semesters. His performance improved in the junior college, and he returned to Texas A&M in September 1941. Hughes was passing all classes when he resigned from the college on December 3, 1941, stating personal reasons. Family members believe that his father was ill and that he left school to assist the family.[3]

Four days later Japanese aircraft bombed U.S. naval forces at Pearl Harbor in the Hawaiian Islands conducted aerial raids on army and air corps installations elsewhere on the island of Oahu. Hughes joined the thousands of young men who quickly began enlisting in the armed forces, enlisting as an aviation cadet on January 28, 1942, in San Antonio. He was twenty years old. After receiving primary pilot training at Tulsa, Oklahoma; basic pilot training at Enid, Oklahoma; and advanced pilot training at Lubbock, Texas, he was transferred to Four Engine Transition School, Combat Crew School, Tarrant Air Base, Fort Worth, Texas. When he completed the prescribed training courses, Hughes received his wings and commission as a second lieutenant, serial number 066629, on November 10, 1942. Two days previously, he had married Hazel Dean Ewing in San Antonio.

In April 1943 at Lowry Field, Colorado, Hughes was assigned to the 564th Heavy Bombardment Squadron, 389th Heavy Bombardment Group. Heavy bombardment squadrons consisted of four flights of three airplanes and crews each. Four squadrons made up a group. The actual number of aircraft in any unit could vary from time to time because of the need for replacements, the current attrition rate, and a number of other factors.

Coming from training schools and air bases across the county, the airmen were assembled into crews and assigned to a B-24 heavy bomber. A crew consisted of four officers — pilot, copilot, bombardier, and navigator — and six sergeants — engineer, assistant engineer, radio operator, assistant radio operator, tail gunner, and belly gunner. The assistant engineer and assistant radio operator doubled as gunners in the waist-gun positions when not needed up front. Hughes's crew was an all-American group of lieutenants and sergeants from places like Refugio, Texas; Wilkes-Barre, Pennsylvania; New York, New York; and the Presidio of Monterey, California. They came from college campuses, high schools, and the workforce and included an actor, a draftsman, a locomotive fireman, and a telephone-maintenance man. Hughes's task was to mold these individuals into an efficient fighting crew. History shows that he did his job.[4]

Their B-24D Liberator, aircraft number 42–40753J, was built at Consolidated Aircraft Company in San Diego, California, one of the 18,482 assembled from 1939 to 1945. The Liberator was an airplane of very distinctive appearance, with its unusually long, thin, tapering mid-wing; stubby, slab-sided fuselage; and very high, oval twin tail fins. Although on the ground appearing huge and ungainly, high in the air it soared with an easy grace matched by few other aircraft. Yet despite its many fine qualities, the Liberator was not suited for low-altitude operations.[5]

Crew training began in earnest in April 1943 at Lowry Field, followed by the movement of the group to Europe. The ground echelon arrived at Camp Kilmer, New Jersey, on June 11 and embarked for England aboard the *Queen Elizabeth*. Leaving Lowery on June 13, each aircraft was heavily loaded with group equipment so that when all ships arrived at the final destination, the unit could set up operations quickly and would not have to wait for items shipped by sea. At the first stop, Lincoln, Nebraska, the aircraft were outfitted for high-altitude combat. Each airman was issued khaki-colored underclothes, heated long underwear with plug-in gloves and socks, bulky fleece-lined leather outer garments, pocket escape kits, life vests, flak vests, and steel helmets; all officers were issued .45-caliber semiautomatic pistols. The next stop was Montreal, Canada, for refueling and rest. The next day the squadron flew to Bangor, Maine, where briefings on the flight over the Atlantic were conducted. The next day the unit flew to Goose Bay, Labrador, the departure point from North America. The next leg of the trip was to Meeks Field, Reykjavik, Iceland, for refueling and rest. Leaving Iceland, the squadron flew to Prestwick, Scotland, and then to their final destination at the Royal Air Force (RAF) base at Hethel in Norfolk, East Anglia, arriving on June 25, 1943.

Crew of the B-24 "Ole Kickapoo." Front row (L to R): Joseph E. Mix, Louis N. Kase, Edmond H. Smith, Avis K. Wilson, Malcolm C. Dalton, Thomas A. Hoff. Back row (L to R): Lloyd H. Hughes, Ronald L. Helder, Sidney A. Pear, John A. McLoughlin.
Courtesy Rebecca Ann Jordan

In his memoir of the war, Capt. Philip Ardery, commander of the 564th Bomb Squadron, writes about the crossing to England:

I picked an excellent crew with the ship I was flying, that of Second Lieutenant Lloyd H. Hughes of Corpus Christi, Texas. Hughes was a laughing, youngish, handsome lad and a much-better-than-average pilot. I had taken Lieutenant Edward L. Fowble out of his assistant-operations job and made him a flight commander of C Flight. This flight consisted of Fowble's crew, Hughes's crew, and the crew of Lieutenant Robert Lee Wright of Austin, Texas. As a patriotic Kentuckian, I was a little jealous of the ascendancy of Texans, but I had to admit that next to Kentuckians, they were about the toughest competitors of all.

I felt that perhaps Hughes somewhat resented my taking over as pilot of his ship for the long hop across the ocean. He was probably a better pilot than I, since administrative duties had recently kept me from flying as much as he did. But I wanted to sit in the pilot's seat and "fly my own ship" across, although it was really Hughes's ship. He took it with good nature.[6]

THE 389TH BOMBARDMENT GROUP (SKY SCORPIONS)

The 389th Bombardment Group was activated on December 24, 1942, at Davis-Monthan Field, Arizona. The group was physically formed at Biggs Field, Texas, on February 1, 1943. The unit comprised four squadrons: the 564th, 565th, 566th, and the 567th Bomb Squadrons. The group began final training on April 17 at Lowry Field and departed for England in June 1943. Upon arrival overseas, the group was assigned to the U.S. Eighth Air Force.[7]

The ten young Americans of Hughes's crew were not aware that their fate was decided already by Winston Churchill and Franklin D. Roosevelt in January 1943 at the Casablanca Conference, where they agreed to bomb the Romanian oil refineries at Ploesti. After the conference the U.S. Ninth Air Force was directed to carry out Operation TIDAL WAVE (code name for the Ploesti raid) sometime between the end of the African campaign and the beginning of the Sicilian campaign. Destroying Romanian refining capacity would help relieve pressure on Josef Stalin's forces defending Russia as well as the Allied armies invading Sicily.

Immediately upon arrival in England, the group began beating up and down the foggy East Anglian countryside in practice flights at treetop level. None of the crewmen knew why, but they reveled in the sudden legalization of buzzing, heretofore a highly illicit practice. English farmers were not happy about the low-level flights over their farms and complained of horses in shock and cows gone dry. To satisfy speculation about this training, the intelligence chief planted a rumor that the intended target was the German battleship *Tirpitz,* hiding in a Norwegian fjord beyond the range of RAF bombers.[8]

The man selected to plan the destruction of the Ploesti refineries was thirty-three-year-old Col. Jacob E. Smart, a West Point graduate and bomber pilot on the staff of Gen. Henry H. "Hap" Arnold, the air corps chief of staff. "You do it," Arnold ordered, and Smart enlisted the best minds he could find to develop the operation: air corps specialists, civilian engineers who knew the workings of refineries, and a British petroleum engineer who had worked at Ploesti before the war.

Several plans were considered, but the colonel believed a low-level raid at 50 feet would inflict the greatest damage. A high-altitude strike would require many more aircraft to achieve the same results, and in 1943 the air corps did not have enough bomb groups to attack Ploesti repeatedly from 25,000 feet.

To the men who would fly the mission, Smart's plan smacked of insanity. The B-24 was a high-altitude bomber, not a ground-attack plane, and the experienced airmen knew there would be terrible losses. Col. John R. "Killer" Kane, commander of the 98th Bomb Group, which would join the Ploesti mission, complained, "It was some wild-eyed dreamer sitting at a desk in Washington who devised the mess of a low-level raid." But Smart would stick by his plan. "Nobody with any sense wanted to fly a B-24 in low, but we had no choice," he said. "It was the only way we could do it. I was about as popular as the illegitimate one at a family reunion." He presented his proposal to high-ranking Allied commanders, including Gen. Dwight D. Eisenhower, chief of Allied operations in North Africa. Air commanders estimated that casualties among the American aircrews could be 50 percent or greater, some believing that they could approach 100 percent. But if the refineries were left in ruins, the mission would be deemed a success regardless of the losses.[9]

On June 30, 1943, the 389th departed England for Benghazi, Libya. When the Sky Scorpions arrived, they came up against the reality of the desert. They found a runway leveled out of the hard, dried soil, and that was about all. There were no facilities around this airstrip, and the men had to pitch their own tents.[10]

Stationed at an airfield called Berka Four, the group flew six bombing missions in preparation for the raid on Ploesti. Hughes's unit, the 564th Bomb Squadron, flew four of them. Their first combat mission was to Maleme Airdrome, Crete, on July 9. This was followed by missions over Italy to bomb Reggio Airdrome on July 11, Bari Airdrome on July 16, and rail yards in Rome on July 19.[11]

The 389th doted on tight formations and equipment maintenance. Despite the fact that most of its ground mechanics still languished in Britain, the air echelon, in its six short raids in the Mediterranean prior to TIDAL WAVE, always put up more planes than were called for in the field order.

The day after the Rome raid, the mission commander, Brig. Gen. Uzal G. Ent, ordered the Ploesti force taken off operations and the sprawl of airfields quarantined. Units began intensive low-level rehearsals. Full-size mockups of the refineries were outlined on the desert floor, with 55-gallon gasoline drums stacked up to simulate smokestacks. For ten days the crews practiced dropping dummy bombs at low level on these simulated targets.[12]

Four days before TIDAL WAVE, a captured Romanian pilot said Ploesti was "the most heavily defended target in Europe," but there was no way to verify this alarming assertion. The mimeograph machines were rolling out intelligence estimates that "the heavy guns would be unable to direct accurate fire at low-flying formations because of their inability to follow fast-moving targets. The results would be nil. The target has been unmolested for years and is not expected to be alert."[13]

Aircrews who would fly the mission were told on July 31 to write a letter home. Each man was to pack up all of his belongings, putting them and the letter on his cot before he took off. If he did not make it back, the letter would be mailed and his belongings shipped home.[14]

On the eve of the raid, Hughes's copilot, Ronald L. Helder, wrote his letter to his parents back in Iowa:

> A few more fairly uneventful days have passed by. We have a few improvements in living conditions since my last letter — having finally finished the Officers Mess building and finished the floor in our tent.
>
> Tomorrow (Sunday) will be a full day for us. The big shots around here say they are going to make us work on the Sabbath and really do humanity a good turn. Turn back your calendar and take a look at August 1st.
>
> We finally named our plane "Ole Kickapoo" because we couldn't agree on a name for it. We have four bombs painted on it to designate raids and four swastikas to designate fighters shot down. Our crew is classified in the best three of our squadron — pretty nifty.
>
> We bought a chicken today and plan on having a chicken dinner tomorrow night. We really have fun swimming in the Mediterranean. This sea is like a crystal clear lake — even flying over it you can practically see the bottom at all times. No subs would hide for long in it.
>
> I'm getting a deep enough tan to pass as an Indian, but have my hair cut like a "Heinie," so I think I can fool anyone anyplace; all I have to do now is grow an English.
>
> Till next time
> Love
> Ronald[15]

THE RAID ON PLOESTI

Ploesti was an oil-boom city at the foot of the Transylvanian Alps, thirty-five miles north of Bucharest. Frequent showers account for its name, which means "rainy town." Its 100,000 inhabitants lived far better than the average Romanian. The city was incongruously fenced by the source of its prosperity—the smoking stacks, cracking towers, pumping stations, tank farms, and noisy railroad yards of eleven huge modern refineries. These were Romania's main economic assets, providing 40 percent of its exports. Ploesti's refineries produced one-third of Adolf Hitler's high-octane aviation gasoline, panzer fuel, benzene, and lubricants. They also supplied half of the oil that kept Rommel's armor running on the sand seas of Mediterranean Africa.[16]

Five bomb groups had been assembled for the raid on Ploesti. The two Ninth Air Force groups based in North Africa, the 98th "Pyramiders" and 376th "Liberandos," were joined by three English-based groups on loan from the Eighth Air Force, the 44th "Eight Balls," 93rd "Traveling Circus," and the new, untried 389th "Sky Scorpions." The mission's planners believed that the low-level raid probably would surprise the Germans, providing an opportunity for precision bombing and reducing the chance of unnecessary civilian casualties. They also thought that a single such raid would be so successful that repeated high-level attacks would not be necessary.[17]

After months of preparations, Headquarters, IX Bomber Command, Ninth Air Force, issued Field Order 58, dated July 28, 1943, designating seven refinery targets, six in the area surrounding Ploesti. The seventh target, designated "Red Target," was the Steaua Romana Refinery located at Campina, eighteen miles northwest of Ploesti. The plan called for a minimum-altitude attack to be made in several waves.[18]

The 389th Bomb Group, because of its relative lack of experience and being equipped with planes with belly turrets (which gave them different flying characteristics), would find it difficult to fly a close formation with the other groups and therefore was assigned the Campina target. Another consideration was that the Sky Scorpions were flying new Liberators with a slightly greater range, and Red Target was the farther objective of the seven. Its isolation from the others called for an individual effort, and the time of the attack did not have to coincide exactly with the main attack.

Steaua Romana (Red Target), owned by the Anglo-Iranian Oil Company, was nestled in a valley of the Transylvanian Alps. The ingenious Scorpions devised their own bombing plan for this complex. The critical part of the target was only four hundred feet wide. Its four vital buildings—boiler plant, power plant, and two still houses—lay in a diamond pattern. Colonel Wood proposed to cross in three waves, hitting each objective three times with bombs graduated from one-hour delay on the first wave to forty-five seconds for tail-end

AUSTRIA

HUNGARY

ROMANIA

BLACK SEA

●Campina
Belgrade ●
●Ploesti
●Bucharest

YUGOSLAVIA

●Sofia

ITALY

BULGARIA

ALBANIA

Foggia●
●Naples

Istanbul

GREECE

AEGEAN
SEA

TURKEY

N

SICILY

CRETE

MEDITERRANEAN SEA

●Benghazi

CYRENAICA

EGYPT

ROUTE OF THE MISSION
TO PLOESTI, ROMANIA

1 AUGUST 1943

```
0      200      400      600      800    1000 KILOMETERS
0    100    200    300    400    500    600 MILES
```

Charlie. The first wave would drive up the diamond, hitting the targets at the bottom and on the right and left. Any remaining bombs would be dropped on the target at the top of the diamond. The second wave would cross obliquely, hitting the bottom and a side target, with any remaining bombs dropped on the other two targets. The third wave would repeat this tactic from the opposite angle.[19]

But the planners were unaware that Ploesti was protected by German general Alfred Gerstenberg, who had spent three years building the heaviest flak and passive defenses in the world. Forty batteries of big guns plus hundreds of machine guns awaited the Americans.

The final briefing was on July 31. The men of TIDAL WAVE were up at 2:00 AM the next morning to prepare for takeoff. Copilots distributed the escape kits to their crews. Each contained a handkerchief map of the Balkans, a British gold sovereign (or a U.S. twenty-dollar gold piece), ten one-dollar bills, and six dollars worth of Greek drachmae or Italian lire—the latter equal to three months' wages for a Balkan peasant. The kit also contained pressed dates, water-purification tablets, biscuits, sugar cubes, and chocolate.

The Scorpions had only skeleton ground crews, and the men who would deliver the bombs helped load their own aircraft. During the night, orders came down to put two boxes of British incendiaries in each plane. The gunners could throw these thermite sticks into the highly combustible refineries as they passed over.

Before dawn on the morning of August 1, the 178 overloaded B-24s queued up for takeoff. Each plane carried at least 3,100 gallons of gasoline and an average load of 4,300 pounds of bombs, bullets, and thermite sticks, exceeding the Liberator's maximum-load allowance. The first, and possibly suicidal, problem of the 2,400-mile roundtrip to Romania was simply to get off the ground. As the bombers gathered at the end of the runways and waited for the dust to settle, tank trucks came around and topped off the gas loads in the regular wing tanks and in the special bomb-bay tanks.

At 7:00 AM tower controllers shot the flares to signal takeoff. The armada climbed to two thousand feet to assemble. Each group was formed of Vs, the basic three-plane units adopted by American heavy bombers in World War II, which permitted the fullest concentration and field of fire for the planes' thirty defensive guns. The Vs were stepped up toward the rear of each group. The men in each plane could talk to each other on the interphone, but there was no talking between aircraft. Command radio frequency was to be silent the whole way to avoid detection by the enemy.

But this precaution was useless since the Germans knew immediately that the force was up from Benghazi. Unknown to Allied intelligence, the Luftwaffe had recently placed a crack signal-interception battalion near Athens, Greece, which had broken the Allies' code and had been reading Ninth Air Force transmissions. Although the attackers were not broadcasting their destination, they had to spread a short, essential message to Allied forces in the Mediterranean theater announcing that a large mission was airborne from Libya. This was necessary to alert friendly air, sea, and ground forces not to jump to the wrong conclusion if a big formation was sighted. Only a few weeks earlier, during the invasion of Sicily, the U.S. Navy had tragically shot down dozens of American troop carriers, mistaking them for German planes.

The flight route took the force to the island of Corfu; across Greece, Yugoslavia, and Bulgaria; then over the Danube River into Romania. As the planes descended after crossing the Danube, the crews began to see the Romanian people and the beautiful countryside. Some men even saw naked girls bathing in a stream. Many of the peasants smiled and waved as the planes passed over.

Things began to go wrong when the lead group took a wrong turn and headed toward Bucharest instead of Ploesti. Once the error was recognized, Ent got on the group command net and announced: "This is General Ent. We have missed our target. You are cleared to strike targets of your choice." With that, individual planes attacked a variety of sites. Some of the refineries assigned to other groups were attacked before the others arrived.

The trailing three groups, including Wood's Sky Scorpions, had turned at the proper initial point, unaware that the lead groups had made an error. The crews would find some of their targets already on fire and have to make their bombing runs through blinding black smoke and deadly fire from enemy flak and machine-gun defenses.[20]

As the Sky Scorpions began their attack on the Steaua Romana Refinery, their aircraft were buffeted by flak and machine-gun fire. Lieutenant Hughes was flying "Ole Kickapoo" in the last formation of his wave. His gunners were firing their .50-caliber machine guns at the flak batteries, at the muzzle flashes of 20-mm guns hidden in haystacks, and other ground targets. The ship arrived in the target area after previous flights had thoroughly alerted the enemy defenses. Approaching the target through intense and accurate antiaircraft fire at a dangerously low altitude, Hughes's plane received several direct hits that inflicted serious damage. Sheets of escaping gasoline soon streamed from the bomb bay and from the left wing. Hughes could have made a forced landing in

B-24 heavy bombers strike oil refineries in Ploesti, Romania, on August 1, 1943.
Courtesy National Museum of the U.S. Air Force,
Wright-Patterson Air Force Base, Ohio

any of the grain fields readily available at the time. The target was blazing with burning oil tanks and damaged refinery installations, from which flames leaped high above the bombing level of the formation.[21]

Captain Ardery, the squadron commander, flying in the same three-ship formation, saw the condition of Hughes's bomber. He radioed the lieutenant to pull up and bail out. Hughes ignored the instruction and held his position in tight formation. With full knowledge of the consequences of entering this blazing inferno, he and "Ole Kickapoo" pressed on into the cauldron.[22] It was the aerial equivalent of Tennyson's "The Charge of the Light Brigade."

> Cannon to right of them,
> Cannon to left of them,
> Cannon in front of them,
> Volley'd and thunder'd;
> Storm'd at with shot and shell,
> Boldly they rode and well,
> Into the jaws of Death,
> Into the mouth of Hell.

Each member of the doomed crew had his own thoughts. Hughes might have been thinking of his family and his young wife. He might have considered that he was just barely twenty-two years old, which is pretty young to die. Or he might have been thinking only of putting his bombs on the target and maybe shortening the war.

Hughes did not elect to make a forced landing or turn back. Instead, rather than jeopardize the formation and the success of the attack, he entered the blazing area and dropped his bomb load with great precision. After successfully hitting the objective, his aircraft emerged from the conflagration with the left wing aflame. Only then did he attempt a forced landing.[23]

Hughes's devoted friend and roommate, Lt. Robert L. Wright, was flying in the same three-plane formation and witnessed the accuracy of his friend's bombing and the crash. Wright had the impression that Hughes was steering for a belly landing in a dry riverbed. He came to a bridge and lifted over it. Coming down beyond the bridge, his right wing caught the riverbank, and the plane cartwheeled to its flaming end.[24]

Captain Ardery gave a slightly different and more detailed version of the event:

> Suddenly Sergeant Wells, our small, childlike radio operator who was in the waist compartment for the moment with a camera, called out "Lieutenant Hughes' ship is leaking gas. He's been hit hard in his left wing fuel section."
>
> I had noticed it just about that moment. I was tired of looking out the front at those German guns firing at us. I looked out to the right for a moment and saw a sheet of raw gasoline trailing Pete's left wing. He stuck right

in formation with us. He must have known he was hard hit because the gas was coming out in such volume that it blinded the waist gunners in his ship from our view. Poor Pete! Fine religious, conscientious boy with a young wife waiting for him back in Texas. He was holding his ship in formation to drop his bombs on the target, knowing if he didn't pull up he would have to fly through a solid room of fire with a tremendous stream of gasoline gushing from his ship. I flicked the switch intermittently to fire the remote-control, fixed .50 caliber machine guns specially installed for my own use. I watched my tracers dig the ground. Poor Pete. How I wished he'd pull up a few 100 feet and drop from a higher altitude.

As we were going into the furnace, I said a quick prayer. During those moments I didn't think that I could possibly come out alive and I knew Pete couldn't. Bombs were away. Everything was black for a few seconds. We must have cleared the chimneys by inches. We must have, for we kept flying—and as we passed over the boiler house another explosion kicked our tail high and our nose down. [Lt. Edward L.] Fowble pulled back on the wheel and the Lib leveled out, almost clipping the tops off houses. We were through the impenetrable wall, but what of Pete? I looked out right. Still he was there in close formation, but he was on fire all around his left wing where it joined the fuselage.

I could feel tears come into my eyes and my throat clog up. Then I saw Pete pull up and out of formation. His bombs were laid squarely on target along with ours. With his mission accomplished, he was making a valiant attempt to kill his excess speed and set the ship down in a little river valley south of the town before the whole business blew up. He was going about 210 miles per hour and had to slow up to about 110 to get the ship down. He was gliding without power, as it seemed, slowing up and pulling off to the right in the direction of a moderately flat valley. Pete was fighting now to save himself and his men. He was too low for any to them to jump and there was not time for the airplane to climb to a sufficient altitude to permit a chute to open. The lives of the crew were in their pilot's hands, and he gave it everything he had.

Wells, in our waist gun compartment, was taking pictures of the grue-some spectacle. Slowly the ship on our right lost speed and began to settle in a glide that looked like it might come to a reasonably good crash-landing. But flames were spreading furiously all over the left side of the ship. I could see it plainly, as it was on my side. Now it would touch down—but just be-fore it did, the left wing came off. The flames had been too much and had

Lloyd Hughes's B-24 in flames while attempting a landing in a dry riverbed near Campina, Romania. Courtesy National Archives

literally burnt the wing off. The heavy ship cart wheeled and a great flower of flame and smoke appeared just ahead of the point where last we had seen a bomber. Pete gave his life and the lives of his crew to carry out his assigned task. To the very end he gave the battle every ounce he had."[25]

Of the ten-man crew, S.Sgts. Edmond H. Smith, waist gunner, and Thomas A. Hoff, tail gunner, survived the crash and were taken prisoner by the Romanians. They remained prisoners of war until war's end. The bombardier, Lt. John A. McLoughlin, also survived the crash but died of burns two days later. Lts. Lloyd H. Hughes, pilot; Ronald L. Helder, copilot; and Sidney A. Pear, navigator; T.Sgts. Joseph E. Mix, engineer, and Louis N. Kase, radio operator; and S.Sgts. Malcolm C. Dalton, waist gunner, and Avis K. Wilson, ball gunner, died in the crash.

The bodies of the dead crewmen were recovered from the wreckage by Romanian authorities and buried in Bolovan Cemetery. On August 2 a "Missing Air Crew Report" was prepared listing the status of each airman. The quick determination of the crew status of "Ole Kickapoo" was made possible by War Department Circular 195, which authorized the commanding officer of the last station of departure to submit a report to the adjutant general that stated whether individual occupants of the missing aircraft should be continued in a missing status or reported as killed.[26]

Two of the seven assigned targets were not bombed, and four were hit by planes from different groups. Estimates were that 42 percent of the total refining capacity of Romania's nine leading refineries was destroyed. One facility, Creditul Minier, was completely destroyed. Later reports stated that Hughes's Red Target did not resume production until after the war. Despite the fact that the mission resulted in heavy damage to the oil facilities, this destruction was not sufficient to be decisive. Except for temporary shortages, the attack did not result in any major decrease in petroleum products for the Germans because they were able to make up the lost production by activating idle capacity and by speedily repairing the damaged plants. Immediately after the raid, they brought in 10,000 slave laborers to begin salvage operations and reconstruction.[27]

Of the 178 aircraft participating in Operation TIDAL WAVE, 162 reached the target area (3 crashed and 13 aborted en route), 51 were lost, and 22 landed (or crashed) at Allied bases on Malta, Sicily, and Cyprus. Of the 89 Liberators that returned to Benghazi that day, only 31 were flyable.

Statistics for those killed, wounded, missing, or captured remain in dispute. Of the approximately 1,620 crew members who reached the target area, 330 were killed, 54 were wounded and returned to Allied or neutral bases, 79 were detained in Turkey, 70 wounded were held in Romania, and 6 were captured in Bulgaria. At the end of the day, 108 men remained behind as prisoners of war in Romania.[28]

In the "cauldron of death" from Campina and Ploesti to the Danube, enemy soldiers and civilians searched the countryside to find any downed airmen. The dead were buried in nearby cemeteries, and the wounded were taken to local hospitals. A lucky few uninjured were taken directly into captivity.[29]

Five Medals of Honor were awarded to airmen who participated in the Ploesti raid. Each member of the crew of "Ole Kickapoo" was awarded the Distinguished Service Cross. Hughes's decoration was later upgraded to the Medal of Honor. The 389th Bomb Group also received the Presidential Unit Citation.

Lieutenant Hughes's posthumous Medal of Honor was presented to his

Lloyd Hughes's widow, Hazel, receives her husband's Medal of Honor from
Lt. Gen. Barton K. Yount at Kelly Field, San Antonio, on April 18, 1944.
Courtesy Thomas and Sharon Ewing

widow, Hazel Ewing Hughes, on April 18, 1944, in a ceremony at Kelly Field
in San Antonio. The medal was presented by Lt. Gen. Barton K. Yount, commanding general of the Flying Training Command.

Early in May 1944, a high-altitude offensive on the Ploesti facilities began,
with 485 Liberators and B-17 Flying Fortresses bombing the refineries and rail-
way yards. The raids continued until August, when the RAF conducted the
final mission on the night of the seventeenth. The aerial campaign against
Ploesti and associated oil targets in Romania came to a close as the Red Army
stormed west into that country.[30]

Years later, on January 26, 1992, Maj. Gen. Philip Ardery wrote in a letter to
a member of the Second Air Division Association:

In response to your letter of Jan. 18, this is to say that I had reason to know Pete very well. He was one of the best pilots of my squadron, the 564th of the 389th Bomb Group. The 564th ultimately was picked as the best squadron in the 2nd Air Division (that is, all of the B-24s in Western Europe). I ranked Pete out of the pilot's seat when we crossed over from Gander to Prestwick in 1943. I recognized his outstanding quality and tried twice to promote him from 2nd Lt. to 1st Lt. only to have my recommendations turned back because "he didn't have enough time in grade." That was just one of the points of disagreement I had with our then Group Commander.

In the book [*Bomber Pilot*] I tell about Pete's heroic mission on Ploesti. I wrote him up for a Congressional Medal of Honor only to have the Group Commander turn it back. But some AP reporters found out about it and some days later the Group C.O. called me in to say that the 9th Bomber Command had found out about Pete and ordered the citation put through. Pete was truly an authentic hero.

I hope this helps you,
Philip P. Ardery
Maj. Gen., USAF Res. Ret.[31]

REPATRIATION AND BURIAL

The War Department directive of December 13, 1941, suspended shipment of deceased military personnel from overseas to the United States. The secretary of the navy issued a similar order.

The repatriation program for the American war dead began as World War II ended. Under the terms of Public Law 383 of the 79th Congress on May 16, 1946, families could request the return of sons and husbands for burial in a national cemetery in the United States or in a private plot. The family could also request that their loved one remain buried with comrades in overseas cemeteries administered in perpetuity by the American Battle Monuments Commission.

Repatriation of the World War II dead was the responsibility of the American Graves Registration Service (AGRS), under the supervision of the quartermaster general. The official program was initiated in the European theater on July 27, 1947. But the operation soon revealed problems and deficiencies that had not been anticipated. For example, the army faced a shortage of licensed embalmers, there were not enough metal caskets available because of the postwar demand for automobiles and refrigerators, and the port of Antwerp, Belgium, had inadequate storage space for all the casketed remains. In response, five transport ships were converted to "mortuary ships" for use in the European theater. In the United States 118 hospital railroad cars were converted to funeral coaches.

Following the end of the war in Europe, negotiations began with the Communist government in Romania to recover the American dead there. AGRS teams could not enter the country without previous clearances, which could take weeks and even months to obtain. Intensified diplomatic action through the Allied Control Commission in Romania soon brought better results. By the autumn of 1945, AGRS units were able to conduct recovery operations there, and the Romanians even helped establish two temporary cemeteries.

The Romanian Detachment of the 347th Quartermaster Battalion (Mortuary), a unit of the AGRS, gathered the remains of fallen Americans from local cemeteries and isolated burial spots and concentrated them at two locations in Romania—the American Cemetery at Sinaia and the City Cemetery of Ploesti. From there, rail connections provided by the Orient Express expedited evacuation to the Central Identification Point at Strasbourg, France. By the close of 1946, a total of 416 American airmen had been recovered. Before these efforts ended in 1947, an additional 78 American dead had been recovered and removed.

At Strasbourg, forensic specialists attempted to identify each set of remains. Those scheduled for repatriation to the United States were prepared for transportation, and those whose next of kin had elected burial overseas were prepared for interment in an American military cemetery in Europe. Rail was the most common means for transportation to the repatriation port at Antwerp. From there the "mortuary ships" provided transportation to the Port of New York, where the remains were placed aboard the converted railcars for shipment to one of the twelve distribution centers located across the country. The distribution center was responsible for delivery of the deceased to the family.[32]

Hughes's long journey home ended when he was returned to Texas in the spring of 1950. He was buried with military honors in Plot 53, Section U, Fort Sam Houston National Cemetery in San Antonio on April 12. Two of his crewmates rest today in the Ardennes American Military Cemetery located at Neuville-En-Condroz, twelve miles southwest of Liege, Belgium. Three others are buried in a common grave in the Fort McPherson National Cemetery at Maxwell, Nebraska.[33]

Lloyd H. Hughes Jr. has been honored in many ways. Williams Air Force Base in Arizona named a building Hughes Hall. On March 1, 1969, a dormitory at Texas A&M University was renamed Lloyd H. Hughes Hall. Lackland Air Force Base has a street named after him. In 1954 Bryan Air Force Base renamed one of its streets in his honor. In 1995 Del Mar College in Corpus Christi added Hughes to its Wall of Honor. His portrait hangs on the wall of the operations room of the 564th Missile Squadron at Malmstrom Air Force Base, Montana. The front hall in the Memorial Student Center at Texas A&M University displays a frame containing portrait of Hughes, a specimen medal, and his Medal of Honor citation. A large bronze bas-relief hangs in the Sam Houston Sanders Corps of Cadets Center. Beneath the plaque is a display case containing the original Medal of Honor and memorabilia from his cadet days at Texas A&M and his military service.

Second Lt. Lloyd Herbert "Pete" Hughes Jr., Class of 1943, was the first Texas Aggie awarded the Medal of Honor.

THOMAS WELDON FOWLER SR.
CLASS OF 1943

"Heroes may not be braver than anyone.
They're just braver five minutes longer."

RONALD REAGAN

THOMAS WELDON FOWLER was born October 31, 1921, in Wichita Falls, Texas, the son of Austin H. and Mattie Wilson Fowler. Austin's first wife, Fanny, died sometime before 1918. Two sons, John William and Samuel A., were born to that marriage. After losing his first wife, Austin married Mattie about 1918, and they had three children, Wilson McKinley, Thomas Weldon, and Charles Nicholas.

Tom Fowler attended Austin Grade School for six years and received honors for citizenship, reading, and not being tardy. At Reagan Junior High School, he played in the school orchestra and was president of the Hi-Y. He was active in the Boy Scouts and attended the national jamboree in Washington, D.C., in 1937. At Wichita Falls High School, he belonged to the Safety Council, Hi-Y, Gym Leaders, and Latin Club. Fowler was also a member of the DeMolay, a Masonic organization for young adults sponsored by a local lodge. Although not particularly of any great philosophical bent, he was an avid student of Latin and history. His favorite books were Edward Gibbon's *Decline and Fall of the Roman Empire* and Douglas Southall Freeman's *Lee's Lieutenants*.[1]

Fowler's father owned an 800-acre farm near Burkburnet, Texas, and in 1930 bought another farm near Floydada. He and his four brothers spent their summers working on the family farms, and the harvest season for wheat usually meant returning to Wichita Falls after the start of the regular school session. At the beginning of one summer, Fowler decided to ride his horse to the Floydada farm. The 170-mile trip took him about a week, an accomplishment for which he was proud. His father died in 1931, but the family continued to operate the farms.

Two of his three older brothers, William and Sam, graduated from Oklahoma A&M College but encouraged Fowler to attend Texas A&M. The six-foot, 159-pound Texan began his freshman year at College Station in September 1939. He selected animal husbandry as his major field of study, believing that Texas A&M excelled in this discipline, according to his admissions application. For his required military-science training, he selected the cavalry branch and was assigned to Troop B, Cavalry in the Corps of Cadets.[2]

Fowler arrived in College Station at the beginning of an exciting year. Enrollment was at an all-time high of 7,177, with more than 6,000 students in the Corps of Cadets. Twelve new cadet dormitories and a dining facility had just been completed on the south side of campus. The football team went undefeated, winning the Southwest Conference. They also won the 1939 National Championship after defeating Tulane 14–13 in the Sugar Bowl. The football team also won the conference in 1940 and 1941.[3]

Thomas Fowler and his fiancée, Ann Oakes, at the Senior Ring Dance, 1943.
Courtesy Thomas Fowler Jr.

During his college years, Fowler continued to court his high-school sweet-heart, Ann Oakes, and invited her to College Station to attend football games and dances. During his senior year, she was in College Station to attend the Ring Dance, which is held after the seniors receive their coveted Aggie ring. As part of the festivities, she turned his senior ring so that the class year and shield on the top of the ring faced outward, indicating that he was a proud graduate of Texas A&M.[4]

Fowler participated in several student activities, including the Saddle and Sirloin Club, Block and Bridle Club, and Wichita Falls Club. He did well as a cadet, serving as a corporal his sophomore year, a sergeant his junior year, and during his senior year, a cadet captain and executive officer of the cavalry squadron. He also served as the student-welfare representative in his senior year.[5]

Everything changed with America's entry into the war. On December 8, 1941, the A&M administration and faculty, as they had done in World War I, pledged their full support to the war effort. The official message from the college to the government was accompanied by a special resolution from the Corps of Cadets signed by the corps commander and directed to Pres. Franklin D. Roosevelt. In early 1942 A&M was once again transformed into an extensive military-training camp. The normal academic structure, class schedules, graduations, and requirements would all change or be eliminated. Pres. Thomas O. Walton and the commandant of cadets, Col. Maurice D. Welty, urged cadets to continue their studies and stay in school as long as possible. They vowed to ensure that any cadet who was drafted would receive credit for work completed, but credit would not be offered if the student quit without an official notice of induction.

After a brief Christmas break, the student body returned in January 1942 to a vastly different campus. The normal two-semester schedule was scrapped for an accelerated year-round program "for the duration of the war emergency." The army wanted more new lieutenants, so graduation of the Class of 1942 was moved to May 16. Once graduation and commissioning exercises were completed in Guion Hall, most of the new officers said goodbye, went directly to the College Station train depot, and were soon en route to their first army assignment.

The wartime academic schedule consisted of three sixteen-week semesters, classes six days a week, and no holidays except for a week at Christmas and a week between semesters. Under this accelerated system, it was possible for a new entering freshman to complete a degree in two years and eight months.

In early 1942 the army, navy, and marines established training courses at A&M, and the U.S. Army Air Corps conducted a civil pilot-training program at Easterwood Airport. Many of the new arrivals were perplexed by the Aggies and their customs. Interactions between the cadets and the military trainees went fairly smoothly, though occasional problems did surface, such as when navy recruits rooted for the Texas Christian University football team at Kyle Field. The clash of cultures was soon overcome as events around the world placed demands on everyone in training on campus.[6]

Fowler graduated from Texas A&M in February 1943 with a degree in animal husbandry. At graduation time the Class of 1943 had not completed the ROTC requirements for commissioning, primarily because those cadets had not attended the ROTC Summer Camp. The graduates were inducted into the army and ordered to their branch Officers Candidate School (OCS) for thirteen weeks of intensive military training. Fowler, being cavalry, attended the Armor OCS at Fort Knox, Kentucky. Upon successful completion of the training in May 1943, he was commissioned a second lieutenant, armor. On May 12 he was in Wichita Falls to marry Ann Oakes. Ann had relatives living in Tennessee, and this allowed her to spend some time with her husband after he was commissioned at Fort Knox. Their son, Thomas W. Fowler Jr., was born on February 17, 1944.[7]

Apparently, Fowler was assigned to a military post in Alabama after his training at Fort Knox. He later shipped out from Fort Dix, New Jersey, in October 1943 and spent some time in North Africa. In February 1944 Fowler received orders to Italy as a replacement officer. After arriving in the Salerno area, he took the opportunity to visit an older brother, Wilson, who was a captain commanding a quartermaster truck company there and later in Anzio. They met up again after Fowler was transferred to the Anzio beachhead and assigned to the 191st Tank Battalion, which was engaged in heavy fighting. The two brothers planned to meet in Rome after it was captured, but fate intervened.

Fowler's oldest brother, William, managed the family farms during World War II and was given an exemption. Another older brother, Sam, had a civil-engineering degree and was commissioned in the U.S. Navy. He served as a lieutenant commander in a naval construction battalion in the Pacific. Fowler's younger brother, Charles, was also in the Pacific serving in the army air force. Charles attended Texas A&M, Class of 1948, after the war.[8]

Shortly after arriving in the Anzio area, Fowler wrote to his wife about conditions on the beach.

8 Mar 44
Anzio
My Precious,
Well, since my last letter, I have changed addresses. I am at the beachhead and it isn't much different from anywhere else except the noise and we live in dug-outs. It is much more fun than being around in a Repl. depot.

Please do not worry about me for there is no reason. You should see our "hole." There are three of us in it. It is about ten feet by four-and-a-half feet deep. It is very comfortable considering where we are.

This unit is really a good one. The men are well trained and know their stuff.

We did have a little excitement one day, though. Jerry dropped about a dozen shells right in our area. No one was hurt. You should have seen us hit the dirt. I never really knew the ground was so close.

We could hear the thing coming and knew it was going to be close from its sound. It was; but I beat it to the ground by a couple of seconds and then after it went off I made it to the nearest hole and got as low in it as possible.

There is a lot of humor in these damn shellings, believe it or not. The things the men say after it is over is amusing. However, suits me if they don't try it anymore!

With all my love,
Your husband
Thomas

On the reverse of the second page of the letter was a note reading, "Precious — I forgot to mail this — That is I misplaced it and found it today. April 26, '44 love Tom."[9]

191ST TANK BATTALION

The 191st Tank Battalion was activated at Fort Meade, Maryland, in February 1940, with the transfer of four tank companies from National Guard divisions (the 26th, from Massachusetts; the 27th, from New York; the 29th, from Virginia; and the 43rd, from Connecticut). Companies A, B, and C were equipped with the M3 Lee medium tank. Company D was equipped with the M5 Stuart light tank. Each company was organized into three platoons of five tanks. A captain commanded each company, and lieutenants served as platoon leaders. Commanded by a lieutenant colonel, the battalion consisted of 750 officers and enlisted men.[10]

The 191st began training in March 1940 with only eight tanks. The earliest exercises involved crews walking through tactical problems until their tanks arrived, the last coming in shortly before the Louisiana Maneuvers of August 4, 1941. Two months of training in Louisiana were followed by maneuvers in South Carolina, after which the unit returned to Fort Meade for more training. Their next stop was the Desert Training Center in California. Desert training was completed in October 1942, at the end of which the unit was ordered to turn in their obsolete M3 tanks for replacement with new M4 Sherman medium tanks.

Leaving California, the battalion moved by rail to its new post at Fort Benning, Georgia, sharing an old Civilian Conservation Corps camp with the 764th Tank Battalion. Training continued, then the battalion was alerted for overseas movement on February 1, 1943. The 191st staged at Fort Dix, New Jersey, then departed for North Africa from New York on February 28 aboard the *Andes,* formerly a British passenger ship pressed into service as a troop ship. Because of the vessel's speed, it did not steam in convoy, and the tortuous zigzag voyage across the Atlantic was characterized by sloppy weather, bad food, and worse quarters. Arriving in North Africa on March 9, the unit began training near Port Lyautey, Morocco, but operations ended before the unit was committed to combat. Amphibious training was conducted in preparation for the invasion of Italy, and the battalion landed under fire at Salerno on September 9 in support of the 36th Infantry Division. After the invasion, the unit was usually in support of the 45th Infantry Division but at times supported the 3rd, 34th, and 36th Infantry Divisions; the 1st Armored Division; and the U.S.-Canadian 1st Special Service Force.

In early January 1944 the battalion moved to a staging area southeast of Caserta preparatory to the amphibious operation at Anzio, participating in that landing initially attached to the 1st Armored Division. The fighting in the Anzio beachhead continued until the breakout in May. After the breakout and the capture of Rome, the battalion was withdrawn from the front lines and marched back to an amphibious training area to prepare for its third amphibious operation. The 191st landed in the initial assault between St. Maxime and St. Raphael in southern France on August 15, 1944.

The battalion fought its way through southern France and crossed the Rhine River on March 25, 1945. The unit was supporting the 45th Infantry Division when the German concentration camp at Dachau was liberated on April 29. Shortly afterward, it was ordered to continue the advance to Munich, Germany, and was there when the war in Europe ended on May 8. During battles in France and Germany, the 191st was attached, at various times, to the 36th, 42nd, 45th, and 79th Infantry Divisions. By war's end the battalion had earned campaign streamers for Naples-Foggia, Anzio, Rome-Arno, Southern France, Ardennes-Alsace, Rhineland, and Central Europe. It had participated in am-

M4 Sherman tanks unload from an LST at the Anzio beachhead.
Courtesy 1st Armored Division Museum, Baumholder, Germany

phibious landings at Salerno, at Anzio, and in southern France. The battalion also received a Meritorious Unit Commendation for the period August 15–November 8, 1944. When the 191st was inactivated on December 7, 1945, at Camp Patrick Henry, Virginia, the organic companies were returned to their states of origin.[11]

THE BREAKOUT AT ANZIO

After the successful Allied landings at Salerno on September 9, 1943, the Germans stopped the advance of the U.S. Fifth Army and the rest of the Allied forces at the Gustav Line. Allied commanders decided to outflank the Germans by landing at Anzio on January 22, 1944. The initial invasion force consisted of the U.S. 3rd Infantry Division, accompanied by detachments of rangers and paratroopers, and the British 1st Division. The U.S. 45th Infantry and 1st Armored Divisions were to follow ashore, prepared to move quickly in continuation of the attack. The invasion caught the Germans by surprise, but they quickly sent forces from Yugoslavia, Germany, France, and northern Italy to occupy the hills overlooking the beachhead. By the end of the first day, 27,000 Americans, 9,000 British, and 3,000 vehicles were ashore.[12]

Few foresaw a bitter, four-month struggle just to retain the beachhead. The stalemated Allies battled desperately on three separate occasions against fanatically attacking Germans with orders from Hitler himself to eliminate the beachhead completely, destroying or capturing its defenders. Few contemplated the fruitless, holding warfare of a World War I style: soldiers standing for hours and days at a time in water up to their ankles or crouching in their foxholes in the daytime because of the almost complete lack of defilade; front lines that faced each other at distances no greater than fifty yards; and above all, the devastating artillery barrages from guns up to and including 280-mm artillery pieces that were apt to land at any time on any part of the position.

The beachhead, in the form it finally assumed following the main German counterattack on February 16–19, comprised an area of little more than a hundred square miles, being about ten miles deep and fifteen miles wide in its greatest dimensions. The Allied forces there included the U.S. 34th and 45th Infantry and 1st Armored Divisions; the British 1st, 5th, and 56th Infantry Divisions; U.S.-Canadian Special Service Force; and the 504th and 509th Parachute Infantry Regiments as well as supporting tank and artillery battalions — in all about 100,000 soldiers.[13]

After four months of intensive combat, the final attempt to break out of the narrow and crowded beachhead was made on May 21 in conjunction with attacks by Allied forces on the Gustav Line. Attached to the 45th Infantry Division, Companies B and C of the 191st Tank Battalion attacked Carano, working through very heavy minefields. German resistance was fanatical, and casualties were heavy on both sides. The commander and the executive officer of the 191st were wounded during this action.

At this time Fowler was serving as a liaison officer to an infantry regiment, believed to be the 157th Infantry Regiment, in the 45th Infantry Division. He was on foot when he came upon two completely disorganized infantry platoons held up in their advance by an enemy minefield. The lieutenant immediately took command and reorganized the units.

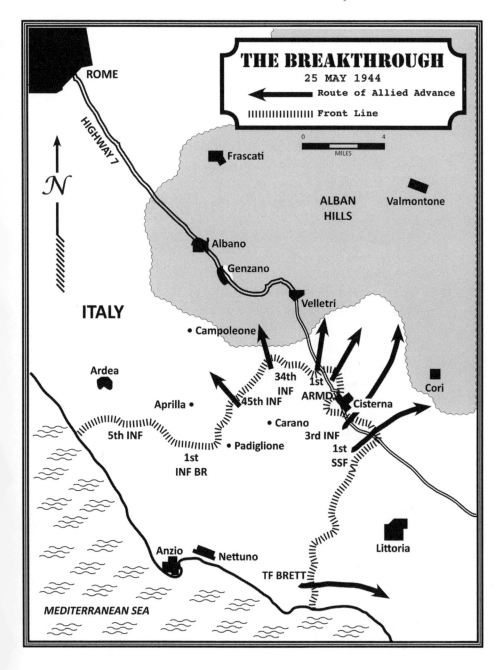

He then made a personal reconnaissance through the minefield, clearing a path as he went by lifting the antipersonnel mines out of the ground with his hands. After going through the seventy-five-yard belt of explosives, he returned to the infantrymen and led them through the minefield one squad at a time.

As the infantry deployed, Fowler made another reconnaissance into enemy territory in search of a route to continue the attack. He then returned through the minefield and led the tanks through to a position from which they could best support the infantry. Acting as a scout three hundred yards in front of the infantry, Fowler led the two platoons forward until he had reached the objective. As he moved forward, he came upon several dug-in enemy soldiers. Having taken them by surprise, the lieutenant dragged them out of their foxholes and sent them to the rear as prisoners. Twice, when he met resistance, he threw hand grenades into enemy dugouts, killing the occupants.

Realizing that a dangerous gap existed between his company and the unit to his right, Fowler continued his advance until the space was closed. He reconnoitered to his front; brought the infantry into position, where they dug in; and under heavy mortar and small-arms fire, brought the tanks forward. A few minutes later the enemy began an armored counterattack. Several German Mark IV tanks fired their cannons directly on Fowler's position and set one of the American Shermans afire. With utter disregard for his own life and with shells bursting near him, the lieutenant ran directly into the enemy fire to reach the burning vehicle. For a half hour, under intense fire from the advancing tanks, Fowler remained in his forward position, attempting to save the lives of the wounded tank crew. Only when the enemy tanks had almost overrun his position did he withdraw a short distance and personally rendered first aid to nine wounded infantrymen amid relentless incoming fire.[14]

The following day Fowler's actions were discussed at his battalion headquarters with pride and amazement. A recommendation for award of the Medal of Honor was prepared by Capt. Edward L. Warner, the battalion adjutant.[15]

After his heroic acts at Carano, Fowler turned down an offer to spend a few days in a rest camp behind the lines. On June 3 he was assigned to Company B as leader of the 3rd Platoon, which was supporting the 168th Infantry Regiment, 34th Infantry Division. At that time Sgt. Oscar L. Smith was acting platoon leader, having lost several platoon leaders either killed or wounded. Fowler reported to his command that morning, and Smith remembers him as a "gung ho" officer. The tank platoon was positioned behind a low rise, with the Germans on the other side. Later that day Fowler said that he was going to

Ann Fowler and Thomas Jr. view photo of Lieutenant Fowler.
Courtesy Thomas Fowler Jr.

make a personal reconnaissance to see what he and his men were up against. Smith told him there was no need to do that since they already knew what was over the rise — German tanks and 88-mm guns.

Undeterred, Fowler mounted a tank and moved out, crossing over the crest. A few minutes later Smith heard a loud explosion and immediately thought that Fowler's vehicle had been hit. After a few more minutes, the tank's driver radioed that he was returning to the area and that the lieutenant was wounded. When he returned, the driver stated that once over the crest, Fowler had opened the turret hatch, and as he stuck his head out, he was shot by a sniper. Fowler died as the tank returned. Sergeant Smith remained with the platoon and was later given a battlefield commission, ending the war in Munich, Germany, as a captain commanding Company B.[16]

Two months after Fowler was killed in action, his widow received a letter from 1st Lt. Ralph W. Carr Jr., an officer serving in Company B, 191st Tank Battalion:

July 18, 1944

Dear Mrs. Fowler,

Please allow me to extend to you my deepest sympathies in the death of your husband Tom. In the short time that I had known him, he had become one of my closest friends.

We are all proud of Thomas and the work that he did before he was killed. Perhaps his brother has already written to you about the brave things that he did. I know that you are proud of him. Thomas was a soldier and a gentleman and he seemed to know better than most of us what we were fighting for. He died that you people back home would never see or feel the suffering that we have seen.

Please allow me again to extend to you and his baby my deepest sympathy. If there is anything I can do or any question I might be able to answer, don't fail to write and ask me.

Sincerely,

Ralph W. Carr Jr.[17]

On November 11, 1944, the Medal of Honor was presented to Anne Fowler and their son, Thomas Jr., at Fort Sill, Oklahoma, by Maj. Gen. Ralph Mc-Pennel. Thomas Jr. wore a child's military uniform at the ceremony.[18]

REPATRIATION AND BURIAL

Prompt identification and evacuation of the fallen was essential to the morale of the soldiers. Each combat company had an officer responsible for burial and graves registration as an additional duty. His task was to identify the dead and organize the evacuation of all remains to a collecting point behind the front lines. From that point the remains were transported to the division collecting point. A platoon from a quartermaster graves-registration company was normally in support of a division, and graves-registration personnel operated a division cemetery in each division's sector. Despite the difficulties of transportation over the rugged Italian terrain, stationary warfare favored efforts to restrict the number of isolated burials. It also offered opportunities for the identification of unknowns that seldom applied in a campaign of rapid movement.[19]

After his death Fowler was temporally buried in the American military cemetery at Nettuano, where his brother Wilson visited the grave in early June shortly after the liberation of Rome.

In preparation for the repatriation of the American dead from southern

Italy, exhumed remains from the various cemeteries were transported to the central casketing point located at Naples, the repatriation port. After undergoing mortuary procedures, the caskets were held in above-ground storage, always totally covered by canvas. In the storage area casketed remains were subdivided into three sections. One of these contained those destined for return to the United States and was further subdivided by the stateside distribution centers. The second section included those scheduled for permanent overseas burial, while the third section was reserved for remains in an unresolved status.

On June 28, 1948, when the first group of deceased departed for the States, a formal ceremony was held at Naples in observance of the solemn occasion. As the USAT *Carroll Victory* pulled away from the pier with its cargo of 4,841 American dead, the cruiser USS *Juneau,* lying in the outer harbor, fired a twenty-one-gun farewell salute.

After the initial shipment, disinterment continued throughout southern Italy, and remains flowed into the Naples center until August 20, when casketing activities ended. Nearly 22,000 casualties moved through Naples during the entire period of the operation.[20]

Fowler was returned to the United States aboard the USAT *Carroll Victory,* which arrived in New York on July 6. His remains were placed aboard a mortuary train and transported to the U.S. Army Quartermaster Depot in Fort Worth, Texas, the closest distribution center to Wichita Falls. From Fort Worth, the casket was shipped by rail on July 26 to Wichita Falls for burial. Fowler was buried with military honors at Crestview Memorial Park on July 27, 1948.[21]

Thomas Weldon Fowler has not been forgotten. American Legion Post 169 and an elementary school in Wichita Falls are named for him. The U.S. Navy christened a coastal tanker, YOG 107, the *Lt Thomas W. Fowler.* An OCS barracks was dedicated as Fowler Hall at Fort Knox, Kentucky. A dormitory on the campus of Texas A&M University is named in his honor, and the Memorial Student Center displays a frame with an artist's rendition of Fowler, a specimen medal, and his citation for the Medal of Honor. A large bronze bas-relief plaque hangs in the Sanders Corps of Cadets Center. Beneath the plaque is a display case containing the original Medal of Honor and memorabilia from his cadet days at Texas A&M and his military service.

Second Lt. Thomas Weldon Fowler, Class of 1943, was the second Texas Aggie to be awarded the Medal of Honor.

GEORGE DENNIS KEATHLEY

CLASS OF 1937

"I had to turn away, for I had witnessed the death of the bravest and most heroic man I had ever known."

T.SGT. CHARLES J. DOZIER, COMPANY B, 338TH INFANTRY REGIMENT

OLNEY IS A rural community in north central Texas located one hundred miles west of Fort Worth and forty miles south of Wichita Falls. It was first settled in 1879 as a place for the annual roundups held by local ranchers. Incorporated in 1909, the town began to grow after 1923, when oil was discovered. By 1930 the population had grown to about 5,000. But the Great Depression brought a decline in the town's size, and the 2000 census listed 3,396 people living in Olney. The town is now an agricultural center, with wheat, cotton, cattle, sheep, and hogs the primary products. Petroleum continues to play an important part in the local economy.[1]

One of its most notable sons, George Dennis Keathley, was born November 10, 1907, to William F. Keathley and Bertha Mary Leberman Keathley on a farm two miles south of Olney. His father came from Tennessee to Olney to teach in a one-room school. His mother was twelve years younger than her husband and, at one time, one of his students. After Bertha inherited a 640-acre farm from her German-immigrant parents, the family moved out of Olney, and William gave up his teaching job to become a farmer. He raised cotton, wheat, cattle, and hogs, and his children did their share of chores on the farms.

George Keathley attended school in Olney but left high school before graduating to move to Lawton, Oklahoma, to live with his older brother, John A. Keathley, Class of 1925. John was operating a meat market on the Fort Sill Military Reservation at the time and later owned a meat market in Lawton as well as a hog farm and meat-packing plant in the vicinity. George worked for his brother and completed his high-school education in Lawton. Continuing to work and paying his own way, he enrolled in Cameron State School of Agriculture and Junior College in town. He graduated from junior college on May 14, 1930, with an associate degree in agriculture.

Keathley applied for admission to Texas A&M and was admitted for the fall semester of 1933 with agriculture as his academic major. He stated in his application that he expected to pay most of his school expenses and to work as much as possible while enrolled. He also received some financial support from his brother John.[2]

In his application for admission, Keathley selected the cavalry branch for his required military science and was assigned to Troop D, Cavalry in the Corps of Cadets. The 1934 *Longhorn* gives his rank as private, and the 1935 yearbook shows him as a sergeant in Troop D.[3]

Like many students working their way through college during the Great Depression, Keathley was forced to withdraw for financial reasons, in his case during the spring of 1935. Even thought he had dropped out of college, Keath-

George D. Keathley with wife, Inez, and stepdaughters Helen (front row) and Paula.
Courtesy Paula Roy

ley did not give up his desire to graduate from A&M. He attended summer school in 1936, 1939, and 1940.

He was fortunate to find employment with the newly formed Soil Conservation Service. According to family members, he had a long-held desire to do something about soil erosion and to improve farming methods. Working for the service provided him that opportunity. Originally assigned to Dalhart, Keathley was soon transferred to the office in Lamesa. At the time the Lamesa office was supervising soil-erosion projects and other programs of the Civilian Conservation Corps (CCC). The CCC was created in 1933 as a result of a need during the Great Depression to put young men to work. A company of the CCC was located in a camp at the south edge of town.[4]

While living and working in Lamesa, Keathley met and later married Inez Edmunson. With the marriage on April 12, 1942, he acquired an instant family with two daughters, Paula Jean and Helen Joy.[5]

Keathley volunteered for induction in the army and entered the service on

May 15, 1942. He arrived at the reception center in Fort Sill, Oklahoma, the following day. From there he was shipped to Camp Shelby, Mississippi, and assigned to the 338th Infantry Regiment, 85th Division. Keathley completed his infantry training at Camp Shelby and participated with his unit in maneuvers in Louisiana and South Carolina. In June 1943 his unit was in Camp Pilot Knob, California, for training at the Desert Training Center. He spent August to October at Camp Coxcomb, California, participating in additional desert training. Keathley's natural ability at leadership earned the soft-spoken Texan a promotion to corporal and eventually sergeant. In 1943 he was promoted to staff sergeant and was one of the leading noncommissioned officers in 1st Platoon, Company B. The training was brought to an end by orders transferring the division to Fort Dix, New Jersey, the last move before shipment overseas.[6]

338TH INFANTRY REGIMENT

The 338th Infantry Regiment was organized on August 30, 1917, at Camp Custer, Michigan, and assigned to the 85th Infantry Division. The regiment served in France during World War I but did not participate in any combat operations. After the armistice the unit remained on occupation duty in Germany. But by August 1919 the 338th had returned to the United States and been demobilized.

The regiment was reconstituted on June 24, 1921, in the Organized Reserves. It was ordered to active military service on May 15, 1942, and reorganized at Camp Shelby, Mississippi, as one of the three infantry regiments in the 85th Infantry Division, the "Custer Division."[7]

A U.S. Army infantry regiment of World War II was organized into a headquarters company, service company, cannon company, antitank company, and three infantry battalions. It had 3,068 officers and enlisted men and was commanded by a colonel. Each battalion contained a headquarters company, three rifle companies, and a heavy-weapons company. Commanded by a lieutenant colonel, a battalion had thirty-five officers and 825 enlisted men. A rifle company contained three rifle platoons and a weapons platoon. It was commanded by a captain and had six officers and 187 enlisted men. Each rifle platoon had three squads of 12 men each and was commanded by a lieutenant.[8]

The regiment sailed with the 85th Division from Hampton Roads, Virginia, to North Africa in December 1943, landing at Casablanca, French Morocco, on January 2, 1944. After arriving in North Africa, the regiment moved to Port aux Poules near Oran, Algeria, for amphibious training.

Allied forces invaded Italy in September 1943, with the U.S. Fifth Army landing at Salerno on the ninth. Another amphibious landing was made at Anzio on January 22, 1944, but Allied forces were confined to the beachhead for five months. In May the long-awaited breakout was accomplished with a major assault on the German's fortified positions.

The regiment sailed from North Africa and on March 27 landed at Naples, where preparations were made to go into the line near Minturo, about forty miles to the north.[9] A few days later, on April 2, Keathley wrote his family about his first impressions of Italy.

> Dear Folks,
>
> Know you would think it an April Fools joke if I had written you yesterday so am holding it over until today. Yes it has been a long time since I wrote you but always ask mother to drop by and say hello for me. Have so little time for writing any one.
>
> Have moved once more and am now somewhere in Italy. Was a beautiful country before the war, but now it is really wrecked. Complete homes blown to bits, bridges blown down, wrecked railways, plenty of trucks, cars, and busses burned. In hamlets, towns, and cities there is great damage done. Don't know if it was by bombs, artillery, or just what, but regardless of that it is a good job and whatever was used was to a great success.
>
> People are on starvation. Both young and old are begging for food, clothing, and cigarettes. Malnutrition is present in children. Most all of them are bloated and have sores on face, feet, and hands. Is plenty to make me realize what I am fighting for. Am well & feeling fine.
>
> Lots O' Love,
> George[10]

On April 10 the 85th Infantry Division was committed to action as a unit for the first time in its history when it faced the formidable defenses of the Gustav Line. The Allies attacked on May 12 and met fierce resistance from the dug-in Germans. In bitter fighting, several infantry companies lost from 40 to 50 percent of their men. The enemy mounted several counterattacks, but by noon of May 15, the last had been beaten off and the Gustav Line broken. The 338th Infantry Regiment attacked that afternoon, seizing Monte Penitro and reducing important enemy strongpoints in Santa Marie Infante.

Enemy resistance now cracked everywhere. The Germans had neither the forces nor the time to establish a new line in front of the 85th. The last desperate resistance on the central Italian front at Cassino was wiped out on May 18, and in the west the final push was underway to join with the forces from the Anzio beachhead.

After clearing out a few pockets of resistance in the Gaeta Peninsula with little difficulty, the 338th enjoyed a short rest. Billeted briefly in what remained of the villas along the coast, the troops had a chance to swim in salt water, get a change of clothes, and replace damaged equipment. On May 21 Keathley's battalion moved by DUKWs (2.5-ton amphibious trucks) to Sperlonga, about twelve miles west of Gaeta. The enemy had withdrawn from the landing area, and the battalion proceeded immediately by DUKW and on foot to rejoin the regiment near Fondi.

By May 26 almost all traces of enemy resistance had disappeared. Forces pushing out from the Anzio beachhead had joined other Allied units coming from the east. As a result, the 85th Infantry Division had been "pinched out" of their frontline positions. After forty-nine days of continuous action in the line, the division was withdrawn and went into a reserve position at Sabaudia, formerly a resort on the coast below Anzio.[11]

In a letter to his family on May 25, Keathley wrote:

> Dear Bud and families,
> Received your good letters and also my dues card for the Aggie. Surely was glad to hear from you once more. Am catching lots of hell over here but think it will be worth all of it to win this war and come back home. Don't care for this country. Am gradually seeing it. Walking forward most every day. We are really pushing forward. Each strong point only detains us a day or so. These Jerries really give us good target practice. After my first shower of machine gun bullets I can knock them down with pleasure. Is a game of get or be got and so far I have been getting. Most of this war though is fought with artillery. Very little small arms fire goes on. Only to clean out the stragglers. We are getting lots of prisoners.
> I am feeling fine. Manage to stay well and going after them. Just hope I can see all this through and come back safe and sound. Hope business holds for you. Marlin stay with the Navy if you have to come in.
> Lots O' Love,
> George[12]

On May 30 the 338th was back in the line and pushing toward Rome. Keathley was awarded the Bronze Star with Valor Device during this period. His citation reads: "For heroic achievement in action on 30 May 1944 in Italy. When his platoon leader was wounded and out of action, Staff Sergeant Keathley

Soldiers of the 338th Infantry Regiment entering Rome on June 5, 1944.
Courtesy National Archives

took command and exposed himself many times to enemy small-arms fire in order to reorganize the platoon which had suffered severe casualties upon contacting the enemy."[13]

The Eternal City, Rome, was of little strategic importance in the campaign. But the psychological significance of its fall was profound, for it would be the first Axis capital captured by the Allies. When the breakthrough to Rome came, it was promptly eclipsed in the world's attention by the D-Day landings in Normandy.

The 338th entered Rome on June 5. Everywhere the people ran out into the streets, shouting and cheering to hug and kiss and shake hands with the marching soldiers. They ran beside the jeeps and trucks, chattering and laughing unrestrainedly, throwing flowers, waving their hands, and some even saluting in the

Fascist manner. It was a spontaneous, happy welcome. After passing through the city, the regiment went to a bivouac area to the northwest.[14]

The day after entering Rome, Keathley wrote:

> Dear Sisters and Families,
>
> No letters since last I wrote so will pass on a little of late news to you. Yesterday we took Rome and I had great pleasure of marching through the old coliseum built by Caesar I believe 1500 to 2000 years ago, saw the old aqueduct used in ancient times to bring down water from the Mts. into Rome, the St. Peters Cathedral, largest church in the world, the statue built by Mussolini and dedicated to Victor Emanuel the II, the stadium and grounds built by Mussolini for Olympic games, the capitol and stood in the square where Mussolini gathered his people and then gazed up to the platform where he stood when he declared war on us. Yes it was all really a treat for a country boy. Today we are 10 miles north of Rome and still going. Hoped to see the Vatican City and home of the Pope, but after all we are fighting a war and had to push on through. This is a fast moving war. We are still pushing and not losing too many men. I am well & feeling fine. Hear from all parts of the U.S. every now and then. It's told to us for second time the invasion [of France] started two days ago.
>
> Lots O' Love,
> Geo.[15]

The division was soon on the move again. Following Highway 2 to the northwest, the men found more and more signs of the routed condition of the Germans, with burnt-out and abandoned vehicles everywhere. Enemy soldiers had fled in anything they could lay their hands on: trucks, busses, motorcycles, and bicycles. The highway wound through gently rolling country, rich pasture land, well-tended olive groves, vineyards, and a few patches of woods. At some places a hill or bluff offered the enemy an opportunity to set up rear-guard positions, and snipers occasionally were found in haystacks. More often than not, contact with the enemy was lost.

On June 10 the division was relieved from the line some forty-six miles north of Rome. The men moved to a bivouac area a few miles south of Rome on the grounds of the Castel Porziano, a large hunting estate belonging to the king of Italy. Here the troops rested before resuming training. The men received their first passes to visit Rome and enjoyed the city they had helped liberate.

The division moved north on June 18 to the vicinity of Leghorn. Still in reserve, its next move was to an area between Volterra and San Gimignano.[16] It was around this time that Keathley wrote a three-page letter to his niece, Katy Kay Keathley, in Lawton, Oklahoma.

> Dear Katy Kay,
> Received your grand letter today. Also letters from Dad and Marlin. . . .
> Now for what war is really like and Katy this is strictly for your benefit since you are the blood thirsty type. I will say though before I start that I have had one other request similar to yours from a little girlfriend, 4 years old. She requested a Jerries leg to make sandwiches. Yes war is all that you have ever seen in pictures and then a lot more added to it. As I told Mary Lou, I have not had a scratch, I mean to amount to anything. Did get the bark knocked off my left leg by shrapnel, but was not serious and I dressed it myself and went on fighting. Have had blood on me from head to foot while dressing other men that were wounded. Have seen men blown to pieces. Others badly mangled, but some have managed to live through it. Saw one man blown half in two and his head and shoulders landed not more than five feet away from me. We were in a mine field at the time and believe me mines can tear a man all to pieces and lay them down in small pieces. Have seen similar casualties from bombs and big shells. Then rifles, machine guns, machine pistols and mortars take still another toll of our boys. Guess I am just lucky, at least so far. Hope to continue to be as lucky.
> So far have received the Infantryman's Badge (highest honor a foot soldier can get and only foot soldiers are entitled to them), the Bronze Star, second only to the Silver Star, for bravery and actions beyond call of duty and will get all the campaign ribbons when they come in. If I had gone to the aid station, I would have received the Purple Heart, but as I said before, I dressed my own wound and missed that one. However, I will carry the scar to remember it by and in all probability would lose the medal. All in all I am not doing so bad.
> Marlin, hope you can continue to hold out. War is rough and have seen plenty of brave men throw down arms and run like scared rabbits when the big ones start falling and covering you with dust and shrapnel. Is not what it is cracked up to be by a damn sight. I personally don't care for medals and glory. I want to come home. . . .
> I am well & feeling fine. Still in rest camp. Thanks for the Aggie. I am receiving my copies now.
> Lots O' Love,
> George[17]

BATTLE OF MONTE ALTUZZO

Monte Altuzzo was part of the Gothic Line, the next major German defensive position that stretched east–west across 170 miles of the rugged North Apennine Mountains. The name evoked the presence of the Gothic kingdoms established in Italy by Germanic tribes in the sixth century. For almost a year, the Germans had been using forced labor to reinforce the natural defensive strength of the mountains with pillboxes, minefields, and tank barriers, particularly along the limited number of mountain roads. The original plan was to attack the Gothic Line through the Futa Pass. Yet intelligence information revealed a strong German presence there, so the main effort was directed instead at Il Giogo Pass, along Highway 6524, seven miles southeast of Futa Pass. Commanders recognized that any successful attack against Il Giogo would require capture of the dominant terrain features on either side of the highway: the Monticelli hill mass on the west (left) and Monte Altuzzo on the east (right). The 91st Infantry Division, spearheading the American drive, was scheduled to reach the outpost line in front of those two heights, there to be relieved by the 85th Infantry Division. The 85th would make the main effort along a narrow front against the dominating peak, the 3,000-foot Monte Altuzzo. The ridge leading to the southern crest of the mountain, Hill 926, included three hills: 578, 624, and 782.

From the peak of Altuzzo, eroding streams had cut north–south spurs and ridges parallel to the planned axis of advance, dividing the terrain into compartments and pockets that provided excellent defensive locations. Heavy stands of pines covered the northwest slope. The ridges were overlaid with rocky soil with low brush or grass. What little concealment there was for an attacking force came from the unevenness of the slope, while the high peaks gave defenders unobstructed observation for miles to the south.

Some enemy positions had been blasted from solid rock, whereas others had been dug into the ground or built of heavy logs. In many locations machine guns had been placed with interlocking crossfire. Barbed wire and antipersonnel mines had been laid across the approaches.[18]

On the night of September 11, the 338th moved by motor convoy across the Arno River at Florence and up Highway 65 to Vaglia, some ten to twelve miles south of the 91st Infantry Division's front lines. The regimental attack order was issued on the afternoon of September 12. All battalions were to move soon after dark to forward assembly areas from which they were to launch the attack at six o'clock the next morning. The 1st Battalion was to make the main effort. All units were at full strength, carried normal allowances of equipment, and

85th Infantry Division soldiers advancing up a trail in the Italian mountains.
Courtesy 1st Armored Division Museum, Baumholder, Germany

had combat loads of ammunition. Five artillery battalions would be in support. First Battalion's plan was to attack in a column of companies — A, B, and C — with one heavy machine-gun platoon of Company D attached to each of the two leading companies.

The men of the 1st Battalion arrived just before midnight at their forward assembly area. Loaded down with full packs and blanket rolls, they had marched on foot for twelve miles up and down hills. After digging in, the soldiers dropped off to sleep. As daylight approached on the thirteenth, the men of Company A, who would lead the battalion's movement to Monte Altuzzo, roused from their short sleep at 4:30 AM, ate K-ration breakfasts, and prepared their equipment for the attack. Leaving their infantry packs behind a farmhouse, they stripped down to the barest gear needed. The night air was cool, and the old field jackets, olive-drab uniforms, and summer underwear in which they had sweltered the day before were no proof against the cold morning drafts sweeping over the hills.[19]

Company A moved out at approximately 6:00 AM and began the difficult climb up the mountain. The first enemy was encountered two hours later when a machine gun fired on a squad crossing an open field. There was little cover or concealment in the area, so the men took shelter in a creek bed. The enemy position was taken under fire by an automatic rifleman, silencing the machine gun. The leading platoon continued to climb the mountain but soon came under heavy mortar fire. Following the mortar attack, the troops continued to advance toward Hill 782. By 1:00 PM the entire company was engaged with the enemy five hundred yards southwest of the crest of Monte Altuzzo. During the afternoon they slowly advanced against sporadic resistance but made little headway.

As darkness approached, the company withdrew to a sheltered position and established a defensive perimeter. By the end of the day, the unit had sustained twenty casualties. On Monte Altuzzo the enemy's defenses were still intact except for the outpost positions that had been knocked out during the day, but these were reoccupied by the Germans overnight.[20]

By mid-afternoon of September 13, the battalion commander had worked out a new attack plan. Keathley's Company B was to leave the forward assembly area at dark and come abreast Company A on Hill 782. Together the two companies were to attack at dawn up the main Altuzzo ridge to the crest of Hill 926.

At 5:45 AM on September 14, Company B moved forward and upward in the renewed attack, soon encountering intense enemy automatic-weapons and

AUSTRIA

HUNGARY

• Milan

ITALY

Venice •

YUGOSLAVIA

• Genoa

MT. ALTUZZO

GOTHIC LINE

• Florence

ADRIATIC SEA

CORSICA

GUSTAV LINE

• Rome

Anzio •

SARDINIA

Gaeta

• Salerno

MEDITERRANEAN SEA

N

SICILY

ITALIAN THEATER

1943 - 1945

0   100

MILES

mortar fire. At 8:30 the company was fifty yards from the top of the ridge, their objective. The Germans then launched a savage counterattack as their snipers infiltrated around both flanks of the forward line. Shortly after that assault was stopped, the enemy launched a second counterattack that was also repulsed.

At 11:30 AM a third counterattack was repulsed, inflicting huge losses on the enemy forces. By this time all officers and noncommissioned officers of the 2nd and 3rd Platoons had become casualties. Keathley, who was the guide of the 1st Platoon, volunteered to take command of the two leaderless platoons, together now numbering twenty men, were also dangerously low on ammunition. Crawling from one casualty to another, he collected their ammunition and administered first aid where possible. The sergeant visited each man of his two platoons, issuing the precious ammunition and giving words of encouragement.

A fourth counterattack was launched by approximately two companies. In a furious charge they attacked from the front and both flanks, throwing hand grenades, firing automatic weapons, and receiving support from a mortar barrage. So strong was the assault that Company B was given up for lost. Keathley shouted his orders precisely and with determination, the men responding to his leadership. Time after time the enemy tried to drive a wedge into the American position, and each time they were beaten back, suffering numerous casualties. Suddenly, an enemy hand grenade exploded near Keathley, inflicting a mortal wound in his left side. Rising to his feet, he fired his M1 rifle with his right hand while holding his torn body together with his left hand. Then taking his left hand away from his wound and using it to steady his rifle, he fired and killed an attacking enemy soldier while continuing to shout orders to his men. For fifteen minutes the sergeant continued to lead his men and fire his rifle. The enemy attack faltered, then finally broke. Their final counterattack had ended in defeat.[21]

Keathley's close friend, T.Sgt. Charles J. Dozier, was an eyewitness: "When the enemy had withdrawn, Sergeant Keathley sank to the ground, his life ebbing away. I rushed to his side and helped him to a sheltered spot on the hillside. He then held up his right arm and asked me to take off his watch, which was a present from his wife, and to send it to her. He became limp in my arms and I saw a cloudy mist come into his eyes. I had to turn away, for I had witnessed the death of the bravest and most heroic man I have ever known, and one man who was undoubtedly responsible for preventing the annihilation of three rifle platoons on the western slope of Mount Altuzzo that day." Dozier also heard Keathley's last words: "Please write my wife a letter and tell her I love her and

I did everything I could for her and my country. So long, Dozier. Give 'em hell for me. I'm done for."[22]

Inez Keathley was informed on October 3, 1944, that her husband was reported missing in action on September 14. On October 16 she received word that he had been killed in action on September 14.[23]

BURIAL IN ITALY

Before his departure for overseas duty, Keathley had told his wife that if he was killed in action, he wanted to be buried where he fought. When given the option of burial overseas or return of the body for burial in the United States, Inez Keathley, following her husband's wishes, opted to leave him where he fought.

George Dennis Keathley rests today in Grave 26, Row 11, Plot D, in the Florence American Military Cemetery. The cemetery is located 7.5 miles south of Florence, Italy, on the west side of Via Cassia. Consisting of seventy acres of gently rolling terrain, it holds the remains of 4,403 American soldiers, most of whom died in the fighting that occurred after the capture of Rome.

The cemetery is set against picturesque, terraced hills beside the River Greve and overlooks a pleasant landscape that includes towering cypresses, gnarled olive trees, and a historic villa. It presents a scene of tranquil beauty. The first interment occurred on April 21, 1949, and by the time the American Battle Monuments Commission assumed control on December 15, 4,353 servicemen were buried there. The final number reached 4,403 by the end of the repatriation program for American war dead.[24]

THE YOUNG COUNTY VETERANS
MEMORIAL CONTROVERSY

In 2000 a monument was erected in Graham, Texas, to honor the veterans of Young County. A committee appointed to establish the criteria for including a name on the memorial adopted the rule that military veterans who entered the service from Young County would have their name on the monument. Citizens were requested to submit names of eligible veterans, and the Keathley family nominated George D. Keathley. After plans for the monument were announced, its leading proponent approached Carla Perry, Keathley's cousin, at her business to solicit a contribution for the project. Perry told him that her cousin's name had been submitted and that he had been awarded the Medal of Honor. About a month later the local paper published an article that listed the names of veterans who would be on the monument. Seeing that Keathley's

George Keathley's grave marker in the American Military Cemetery near Florence, Italy.
Courtesy Florence American Military Cemetery

name was not included, Perry questioned the man who had solicited her contribution. He was adamant that Keathley's name would not be on the monument because he had not entered the service from Young County but instead from Lamesa in Dawson County. This caused some distress in the Keathley family and in the Aggie community in Young County. None of them could understand the decision to exclude a Medal of Honor recipient born and raised in the county.

Many of the Aggie alumni believed that Keathley's exclusion on a technicality was an insult to him, and they began a quiet campaign to have his name placed on the monument. Those in Olney, Keathley's hometown, lobbied the members of the committee from their town to vote to overturn the decision. The Graham Aggies did the same with committee members from that community.

Perry began gathering information and documents about Keathley and submitted her research to the committee, but she did not appear before the group. She thought it ironic that the name of Keathley's brother, Marlin, appeared on the published list and that there was no controversy about his name, especially since he entered the service while living in Lawton, Oklahoma. Indeed, several names on the monument were those of veterans who lived in adjacent Archer County but had been drafted by the Graham draft board. The controversy ended when the committee voted to add Keathley's name. Once the vote was taken, the leading proponent, who had so vocally opposed Keathley's name on the monument, promptly resigned from the committee.

The name of George Dennis Keathley appears today in a position of honor on the Young County Veterans Memorial, thanks to a concerned family and a group of loyal Aggies.[25]

PRESENTATION OF THE MEDAL OF HONOR

On April 11, 1945, a posthumous award of the Medal of Honor was made to Inez Keathley at Camp Wolters, Texas. The slim, dark-haired woman was clad in a simple black suit topped by a gold-colored blouse. She stood erect and composed as Maj. Gen. Bruce Magruder, commander of the Infantry Replacement Training Center at Camp Wolters, near Mineral Wells, Texas, placed the medal, attached to a ribbon, around her neck.

Inez Keathley lifted her head with pride when the citation from Pres. Franklin D. Roosevelt was read. Many relatives and friends from points scattered across West Texas gave way to open tears as the actions of the mortally wounded Keathley in beating off a German attack were recounted. His two

George Keathley's Medal of Honor presented to Inez Keathley at Camp Wolters, Texas, by Maj. Gen. Bruce Magruder on April 11, 1945. Courtesy *Fort Worth Star-Telegram* Collection, Special Collections, The University of Texas at Arlington Library

young daughters, Helen Joy and Paula Jean, along with his parents and brothers John and Walton, attended the ceremony. Other relatives in attendance were uncles, aunts, and cousins. Mrs. Keathley's family was represented by her three brothers and a niece. Troops of the 64th Infantry Training Battalion passed in review following the presentation.[26]

Keathley has been honored in three states. The Veterans of Foreign Wars Post in Lawton, Oklahoma, is named for him. Cameron College, where he went to junior college, has named their Reserve Officers Training Corps Drill Team the "Keathley Rifles." The U.S. Army Reserve Training Center in Lawton is named after Keathley, and the U.S. Army Reserve Training Center in Arlington Heights, Illinois, contains a display honoring him. In 1949 a troopship, USNS *George D. Keathley,* was named in his honor. Keathley's name has been inscribed on a monument to veterans in Lamesa and on the Young County memorial in Graham. Lamesa's Veterans of Foreign Wars post is also named for him. Texas A&M University has a dormitory named in his honor, and the Memorial Student Center displays a frame containing an artist's rendition of Keathley, a specimen medal, and his Medal of Honor citation. A large bronze bas-relief plaque hangs in the Sam Houston Sanders Corps of Cadets Center. Beneath the plaque is a display case containing Keathley's original Medal of Honor, Bronze Star, Purple Heart, and other memorabilia from his cadet days at Texas A&M and his service in the 338th Infantry Regiment.

S.Sgt. George Dennis Keathley, Class of 1937, was the third Texas Aggie awarded the Medal of Honor.

HORACE SEAVER CARSWELL JR.

CLASS OF 1938

Greater love hath no man than this:
that a man lay down his life for his friends.

JOHN 15:13

HORACE SEAVER CARSWELL JR. was born on July 18, 1916, in Fort Worth, Texas, the son of Horace S. Carswell Sr. and Bertha Rea Carswell. The family home was in a middle-class neighborhood on Fort Worth's north side. Carswell Sr. was a longtime employee of Swift and Company, a meat-packing plant near the stockyards.

When Carswell was seven weeks old, the family moved to Justiceburg in West Texas, but by the time he was one year old, they returned to Fort Worth and again lived on the north side. At the age of seven, he entered the first grade at Denver Avenue Grade School. After completing the sixth grade, he enrolled at North Side Junior High School. From September 1931 to June 1934, Carswell attended North Side High School, where he was an outstanding athlete, playing football, basketball, and baseball. He was the quarterback for two years and in 1933 scored the winning touchdown in an Armistice Day game against a tough Wichita Falls team. Because of his compact build, the five-foot-nine-inch, 160-pound Carswell was called "Stump" by friends and classmates. The young man had many interests in high school other than athletics. He was the advertising manager of the school yearbook and active in the Boy's Glee Club, Hi-Y Club, and the National Thespian Club. He won first place in individual acting in the citywide one-act-play contest in 1934. During summers while in high school, he worked at Swift and Company in the mailroom or as a laborer in the plant. He was considered a real daredevil by his friends, always having to jump into the swimming hole from the highest perch and riding the Ferris wheel or roller coaster for the longest number of consecutive times.

In his application for admission to Texas A&M, Carswell stated that the main reason he wanted to go to the college was because of its course in agriculture and the "Aggie spirit." After graduation he planned to be a rancher, thus his decision to select agriculture as his course of study. For his required military-science course, he requested the infantry but was placed in the cavalry instead, assigned to Troop B, Cavalry in the Corps of Cadets.

Carswell entered Texas A&M in September 1934 with the hopes of playing football but did not make the team. At the end of his freshman year, he transferred to Texas Christian University (TCU) in Fort Worth. While at TCU he worked in the shipping department of a local department store to help pay his way through college, but the time spent working delayed his studies. Even with his part-time job, he found time to participate in sports at TCU, where he was a utility player on the baseball team for three years, playing infield and outfield. As a member of the football team, he played with TCU legends and

All-Americans Sammy Baugh, Davey O'Brian, and Ki Aldrich. Carswell was a member of the "T" Association, which was composed of athletes who lettered in any one of four varsity sports. He graduated from TCU on August 26, 1939, with a bachelor of science degree in physical education and a minor in history. He afterward worked for an insurance company in Fort Worth.[1]

On March 26, 1940, Carswell enlisted at Dallas, Texas, as a flying cadet in the U.S. Army Air Corps. He received his primary flight training at the Spartan School of Aeronautics in Tulsa, Oklahoma. Since 1939 the air corps primary-flying schools were operated by civilian companies. These schools used Stearman, Ryan, and Fairchild trainers owned by the army air corps; their flight instructors were civilian employees. Each cadet was given sixty hours of flight training in nine weeks before moving on to basic flight school.

From Tulsa, Carswell proceeded to the Air Corps Primary Flying School at Randolph Field, Texas. The following September he transferred to the Air Corps Advanced Flying School at Kelly Field, Texas, where he completed his final phase of pilot training and was commissioned a second lieutenant, air corps reserve, on November 16, 1940, with a rating of pilot.

After receiving his commission, Carswell was immediately called to extended active duty and assigned to Randolph Field as a flying instructor. His next assignment was at Goodfellow Field in San Angelo, where he received further training. While stationed at San Angelo, he renewed his acquaintance with Virginia Ede, who he had met on a double date at TCU. Her father was the mayor of San Angelo and owner of the Studebaker car agency. Virginia graduated from TCU in 1938 with a degree in home economics. Carswell and Ede were married in October 1941. Virginia once explained some of her husband's actions: "He was happy-go-lucky and always a daredevil, up to kid pranks. He liked to fly low and 'buzz the field,' and when I'd have a bunch of girls at my father's camp on the Concho River, near Christoval, he'd wait until they were all in swimming, then zoom a plane low to scare them."[2]

Carswell was promoted to first lieutenant on February 1, 1942, and in August was assigned to the 62nd Squadron, 39th Bombardment Group at Tucson, Arizona. Later transferred to Biggs Field, Texas, he became a flight commander in September and was promoted to captain on December 8. In January 1943 he was transferred to the army air base at Clovis, New Mexico, and assigned to the 356th Bombardment Squadron, 302nd Bombardment Group as squadron commander. He later served as group commander and deputy group commander until November 1, 1943, when he was transferred to Langley Field,

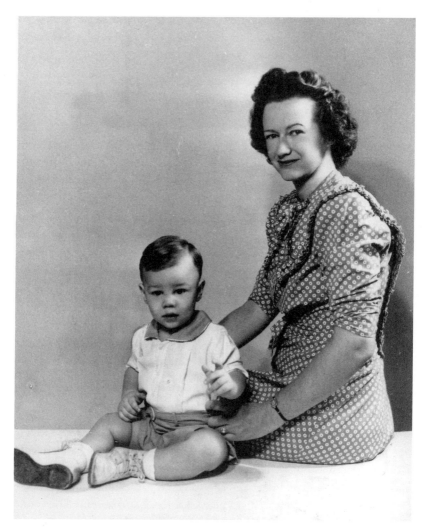

Virginia Ede Carswell with son, Robert Ede. Courtesy *Fort Worth Star-Telegram* Collection, Special Collections, The University of Texas at Arlington Library

Virginia. Carswell was promoted to major on April 23, 1944, and departed the United States on the same day for duty in China with the 374th Bombardment Squadron, 308th Bombardment Group.[3]

308TH BOMBARDMENT GROUP

The army air forces authorized the establishment of the 308th Bombardment Group (Heavy) on January 28, 1942, though the group was not activated until April 15 at Gowen Field, Idaho. That same day the 373rd, 374th, 375th, and 425th Bomb Squadrons were activated and assigned to the 308th Group. For the next three months, little training occurred while the unit worked through its growing pains, resolving administrative and personnel-acquisition difficulties. Then a totally new problem arose when all but four men were transferred to the 330th Bomb Group, a replacement training unit. In September crews were taken from the 39th Bomb Group to form a cadre for the 308th. On the twenty-ninth the group was designated an operational training unit, with Wendover Field, Utah, as its home station. The 308th was fully manned by the end of November 1942.

During this period of personnel turnover, the flying echelon was transferred to Davis-Monthan Field in Tucson, Arizona, for incidental training. The flight crews had been chosen and assigned to the four squadrons. The officers and enlisted men came to the unit as they completed training at their respective schools — pilot, navigator, bombardier, radio, engineer, or gunnery.

Members of the group had to complete three phases of training prior to moving overseas and entering combat. The flying personnel spent most of October in transition training with the B-24 concurrently training their combat crews. Meanwhile, the ground echelon was acquiring, organizing, and processing personnel and supplies at Wendover Field.

With the training completed and the personnel and supplies processed, the 308th officially transferred to China early in 1943. The air echelon began flying its new B-24D Liberators from Morrison Field, West Palm Beach, Florida, on February 15, 1943. The air route took them through Central and South America, the Azores, Africa, and India, while the ground echelon traveled by ship across the Pacific to India.

The group was assigned to Maj. Gen. Claire L. Chennault's Fourteenth Air Force and was initially stationed at Kunming, China. The first order of business was to supply themselves by flying over the "Hump" (Himalayan Mountains) between India and China. Gen. Henry H. "Hap" Arnold, chief of staff of the army air forces, declared that "before a bombardment group in China can go on a single mission in its B-24 Liberators, it must fly the Hump four times to build up its supplies." The B-24s, with their capability to haul huge loads, was suited to double as their own transports for the gasoline, bombs, ammunition, and other supplies needed for combat missions. In addition, the gunners could protect the aircraft from enemy fighters en route and the bombardiers could drop bombs on enemy targets instead of flying empty from China to India. The ferry route over the Hump required flying at altitudes from 20,000 to 25,000 feet, which meant nearly continual bad weather and severe icing conditions.[4]

The 308th supported Chinese ground forces; attacked airfields, coal yards, docks, oil refineries, and fuel dumps in French Indochina; mined rivers and ports; bombed maintenance shops and docks in Rangoon, Burma; and attacked Japanese shipping in the East China Sea, Formosa Strait, South China Sea, and Gulf of Tonkin. The group moved from Kunming to Hsinching on February 10, 1945. It received a Distinguished Unit Citation for an unescorted bombing attack conducted through antiaircraft fire and fighter defenses against docks and warehouses at Hankow, China, on August 21, 1943. The 308th was awarded a second Distinguished Unit Citation for interdiction of Japanese shipping through 1944 and 1945.

In June 1945 the group moved to Rupsi, India, serving with the Air Transport Command in ferrying gasoline and supplies to China. After the end of the war in the Pacific, the men steamed for the United States, where the group was inactivated on January 6, 1946. In addition to the two Distinguished Unit Citations, the 308th was awarded campaign streamers for India-Burma, China Defensive, New Guinea, Western Pacific, and China Offensive.

In his memoirs General Chennault commended the men of the 308th:

They took the heaviest combat losses of any group in China and often broke my heart by burning thousands of gallons of gas only to dump their bombs in rice paddy mud far from the target. However, their bombing of Vinh railroad in Indo-China, the Kowloon and Kai Tak docks at Hong Kong, and the shipping off Saigon were superb jobs unmatched anywhere. When the Army Air Force Headquarters in Washington tallied the bombing accuracy of every bomb group in combat, I was astonished to find that the 308th led them all. Liberators of the 308th dropped the first Allied bombs on Shanghai and Saigon, sounded the first air-raid alarm in Manila after the fall of Corregidor, and earned fulsome praise from Fleet Admirals Halsey and Nimitz for their patrol work over the South China Seas during the Second Battle of the Philippine Seas when they covered the Navy's blind flank.[5]

THE AIR WAR IN CHINA

U.S. involvement in the war in China began when Pres. Franklin D. Roosevelt signed an executive order authorizing American military airmen to resign from their respective services to serve in the civilian American Volunteer Group (AVG), later known as the "Flying Tigers." The AVG was formed and trained to fight for China under the leadership of Claire L. Chennault, a U.S. Army Air Corps captain who had been retired for physical disability.[6]

Chennault had gone to China in 1937 on a two-year contract to serve as an advisor to the Chinese Aeronautical Commission. He quickly earned the respect of Generalissimo and Madame Chiang Kai-shek and was made director of combat training for the Chinese Air Force. In early 1941 he persuaded the U.S. government to send him about one hundred P-40 fighter planes intended for Sweden but that could not be sent there because of the war in Europe. Yet there were no pilots to fly them until Roosevelt's executive order. About one hundred pilots and 150 mechanics signed up, and the First AVG came into being.

After America's entry into the war, the AVG was deactivated and its men encouraged to join the U.S. Army Air Corps. The China Air Task Force (CATF) was activated on July 4, 1942, composed of thirty-five battered P-40s, most of them inherited from the AVG, and seven B-25 Mitchell medium bombers. The CATF received reinforcements from its parent organization, the Tenth Air Force, based in India. At that time, there were no heavy bombers in the CATF.[7]

In March 1943 the CATF was deactivated, and the Fourteenth Air Force was activated under the command of Chennault. Later that month the 308th Bomb Group flew over the Hump into the Kunming area. The 425th Squadron was to be stationed at Kunming; the 373rd at Yanghai, forty-eight miles northeast of Kunming; and the 374th and 375th were to operate from Chengkung, twelve miles southeast of Kunming. After several trips over the Hump to build up the necessary levels of supplies, the group commenced combat operations in China.[8]

Joining the 308th Bomb Group in May 1944, Carswell was first assigned to the group headquarters staff and later to the 374th Bomb Squadron as operations officer. Because of his past experience as an instructor, he flew with different crews of the group to observe pilots' reactions and their proficiency at flying in formation. On these flights he often fulfilled different duties on the aircraft, such as copilot.

Returning from a mission in July 1944, he was forced to bail out when the weather closed in over the Kunming area and his plane ran out of gas. Carswell

SOUTHEAST CHINA

1943

Map not to scale.

B-24s of the 308th Bomb Group, Fourteenth Air Force, escorted by P-40s and P-51s while raiding a Japanese supply point during the Hunan campaign. Courtesy National Museum of the U.S. Air Force, Wright-Patterson Air Force Base, Ohio

ordered the crew to bail out, and he followed. None of the airmen were badly injured in the jump to safety, and after landing, they were assisted by Chinese guerrillas in their trek through the mountains to their home base. Eight days later the men arrived at Chengkung, just in time to stop missing-in-action messages from going out to their families.

After three months of combat flying, Carswell was sent to command a detachment of B-24Js taken from among the group's bomb squadrons. The B-24J was a radar-equipped bomber that could be used for low-altitude missions, in this case primarily for interdiction of enemy shipping in the sea lanes extending from French Indochina to Formosa. The detachment was stationed at Liuchow, four hundred miles southwest of Kunming.[9]

On October 15 Carswell's bomber took off from Liuchow for a night sweep over the South China Sea to search for enemy shipping. About 150 miles east of Hong Kong, his crew sighted a group of six vessels. Diving to four hundred feet in the direction the ships were steaming, the B-24 encountered concentrated fire from the heavily armed vessels. Lining up for a stern-to-bow run, one direct hit and two near misses were scored on a destroyer, which brought it to a halt. More bombs fell in a second run on the ship, which was by now signaling frantically to other vessels for help. When others on the aircraft reported a nearby cruiser, identified as a three-stack *Nagara*-class light cruiser, Carswell decided to make a stern-to-bow bomb run on that ship, dropping three bombs. As the plane streaked over the cruiser amid heavy antiaircraft fire from it and its escorts, there was a blinding flash below followed by a tremendous explosion. As Carswell turned around to look, the cruiser reportedly folded up in the middle and began to sink. Within a few minutes the B-24 turned back and made a final run on a destroyer, dropping its last three bombs, then turned homeward, reportedly leaving this second vessel in a sinking condition. Later that day the U.S. Navy confirmed that two enemy warships had been sunk. Carswell was awarded the Distinguished Service Cross for this action.[10]

Eleven days after his previous successful mission, Carswell scheduled himself with another crew for a sea-sweeping mission. At about 5:15 PM on October 26, the B-24J lifted off and crossed the coast after dark. Carswell and his crew headed down the South China Sea in bright moonlight to locate a large convoy consisting of eight naval and merchant vessels reported southwest of Hong Kong. At about 8:15 PM the radar operator spotted a convoy of twelve ships. Carswell's first bomb run was made from six hundred feet on a destroyer, and he reported to his crew that the six bombs they had dropped had damaged the ship. The enemy force, taken by surprise, did not open fire.

After leaving the immediate area and circling for thirty-five minutes, a second run was made at six hundred feet on a tanker or freighter. Three bombs were dropped, the first landing in the water seventy feet short, but the other two were direct hits. Further observation was impossible, but the vessel was claimed as probably sunk. The enemy force, now fully alerted, met this second attack with a well-directed antiaircraft barrage. The bomber sustained many hits: the No. 1 and No. 3 engines were shot out, No. 2 engine was sputtering, the hydraulic system was out, No. 2 gas tank was leaking fuel, and there were numerous holes throughout the plane. Carswell had great difficulty in righting the aircraft and gaining altitude. He jettisoned the three remaining bombs, and the crew began throwing out everything removable.

About twenty minutes after heading on a return course away from the attack site, someone noticed that the copilot, Lt. James H. Rinker, had a severe wound in his right hand. After Rinker, who had remained at the controls without mentioning his wounds, was removed from his seat and administered first aid, Lt.

James L. O'Neal, the regular pilot of the crew, took the copilot's seat. The other officers in the crew were Lts. Walter H. Hillier, bombardier, and Charles A. Ulery, navigator. The enlisted men in the crew were Sgts. Charles A. Maddox Jr., engineer-gunner; Kaemper W. Steinman, armorer-gunner; Ernest P. Watras, radio operator; Norman Nunes, gunner; Carlton M. Schnepf, gunner; and Adam Hudek, radar specialist.[11]

When the plane crossed the coastline, it was flying at 3,500 feet and having difficulty maintaining altitude. The crew members had expected to bail out upon reaching the coast. When this did not happen, they thought the reason was because Hillier's parachute had been hit by shell fragments and he had refused to jump with a damaged parachute. An hour later, with No. 2 engine sputtering, the plane began losing altitude and would not hold a course, but the engine picked up again, and the plane began to climb. Two or three times it got to 4,000 feet. Fifteen minutes later the No. 2 engine sputtered again, and the plane began losing altitude. Carswell managed to get back to 1,500 feet by straining the remaining two engines to the utmost, bringing the plane up nearly into a stall, then diving a little to regain speed. Realizing their predicament, the crew members (except Carswell, O'Neal, and Hillier) were on the catwalk waiting for the order to bail out. That order was finally given, and at 11:15 PM the eight crewmen jumped from an estimated height of 2,000 feet. The plane was now out of control, with its pilots trying to dodge mountain peaks that rose almost to their altitude. The surviving crew observed the crash by the impact explosion on a mountainside ten miles to the west.

Rinker and Steinman were killed when their parachutes failed to open. The other six landed safely and made contact with a Chinese member of the British Air Aid Group (BAAG). The BAAG was a secret unit organized in southeastern China to rescue downed Allied airman and escort them to safety. The survivors were taken to the Catholic mission at Tungchen. The bodies of Rinker and Steinman had arrived in sealed caskets shortly beforehand and placed in a small chapel. All attended the ceremony in which Catholic rites were given the two bodies before burial on a nearby hillside. On October 31, as the survivors were preparing to leave, three sealed caskets bearing the remains of Carswell, O'Neal, and Hillier were brought in.

The men were not permitted to remain for the burial because their guides were concerned about the Americans' safety. After an arduous trip walking though the mountains and traveling by sampans, the group arrived at Nanning. Several days later they were transported to Kunming and arrived at Chengkung, the home base of the 374th, on November 9. For the selfless act of remaining with his aircraft in an attempt to save two of his crew, Carswell was recommended for the Medal of Honor.[12]

REPATRIATION AND BURIAL

The China and India-Burma theaters comprised the two great land areas of Asia in which significant AGRS activities took place during and after World War II. Although fatalities in these vast regions were far fewer than in the Pacific theater, AGRS faced many problems peculiar to large land areas where the dead were widely scattered.

In China, U.S. forces consisted mostly of technical missions, combat-liaison teams, and widely dispersed air corps units that operated in an area over half the size of the United States. Before the AGRS, China Zone was activated at the end of 1945, the double task of searching for and concentrating American war dead in centralized cemeteries had already begun. During combat operations, the Air Ground Aid Section of the China theater returned survivors of air crashes to their home bases. The 106th Quartermaster Graves Registration Platoon worked with this section, locating and registering remains and graves of scattered American dead, in many cases centralizing bodies into more convenient spots.

Concentration activities during and after the war were fraught with countless difficulties. Often, work proceeded slowly because AGRS technicians either lacked the locations of fatal airplane crashes or the crash sites were inaccessible. In some cases six weeks were required for teams to travel to an isolated burial place, unearth the remains, and transport them to a spot from which they could be moved by air or truck to a military cemetery.

Just before V-J Day, on August 11, 1945, the headquarters of the China theater issued a memorandum that served as a basis for future AGRS operations. It stressed the point that all burials would be made with full realization of their temporary nature and based on the assumption that all bodies would be returned eventually to the next-of-kin in the United States or moved to permanent overseas military cemeteries. The memorandum also included instructions for transporting the dead to the most accessible temporary burial grounds, listing five temporary American military cemeteries in China. Responsibility for the operation of these cemeteries rested upon the base-section commander within whose areas they were located.

A few days later China-theater headquarters recommended to the army chief of staff the activation of three additional graves registration detachments to recover solitary burials and centralize all remains in China either at Kunming or Chengtu. These two locations were chosen because they already contained by far the largest number of U.S. graves in the China theater. Kunming had served as a hub of American military activities and as a base for Chennault's air operations. The centralization of all located remains there or in Chengtu had the additional advantage of simplifying future concentration at Shanghai preparatory to repatriation to the mainland or permanent overseas burial. The total number of remains to be moved to Shanghai included 847 at Kunming and 294 at Chengtu.

The evacuation plan initialized on March 6, 1947, when the first load of remains from Kunming moved by air to Shanghai. On March 19 the AGRS team finished its exhumation task at Kunming and moved on to Chengtu to exhume the graves there. The entire operation had changed abruptly on March 12 when the War Department issued orders to evacuate all deceased personnel in China to Hawaii. Plans to establish a central identification unit in Shanghai were cancelled, and all burials in Shanghai were to be exhumed and boxed immediately. Remains were to be stored above ground awaiting the troopships *General Weigle* and *Admiral Benson,* scheduled to arrive on April 13 and 16. The change in plans was inspired by the increasingly unstable political situation in China.

AGRS teams eventually exhumed and removed a total of 2,583 remains to Shanghai for later repatriation. Search-and-recovery teams remained in China afterward, and by the time the mission ended in 1948, some additional U.S. dead had been shipped from Shanghai to Hawaii.[13]

Following his fatal crash, Carswell was buried at a Catholic mission in Tungchen, China. His family was notified that he was missing in action, remaining in that status until declared killed in action on November 23, 1944. He was moved from Tungchen and reburied in the American Military Cemetery at Kunming, China on October 29, 1945. After the war his body was sent first to Shanghai for repatriation, then to Hawaii, where he was buried on November 15, 1947. On January 19, 1948, his body was disinterred and shipped to the United States aboard the USAT *Cardinal O'Connell.* From California the remains were transported aboard a special funeral train to the Fort Worth Quartermaster Depot, arriving on February 24. The following day his casket was transferred to Shannon's Funeral Chapel on the north side near his boyhood home. Burial was at the Rose Hill Cemetery in east Fort Worth on February 26.

After the Fort Worth Army Air Field was renamed Carswell Air Force Base, he was reburied again on October 9, 1986, in a place of honor on the base. Nine days later the U.S. Air Force dedicated Carswell Memorial Park. Cars-

Horace Carswell monument at the Naval Air Station/Joint Reserve Base (formerly Carswell Air Force Base) in Fort Worth. Courtesy Donald "Buck" Henderson

well's son, Robert Ede Carswell, was present for the ceremony and remarked: "It's a dream come true to me. I've always wanted my father on this base. Flying was his entire life. He belongs here." When the base was closed in 1993, which people thought at the time would be a permanent closing, the body was moved in appropriate ceremonies to Oakwood, an old historic cemetery on the north side of Fort Worth near where he grew up. His parents were moved from Rose Hill Cemetery and reburied beside him. His burial plot, named the Carswell Memorial Park, overlooks the Trinity River and has a view of downtown Fort Worth.[14]

PRESENTATION OF THE MEDAL OF HONOR
The ceremony for the posthumous award of the Medal of Honor was held at Goodfellow Field in San Angelo on February 27, 1946. Carswell's son, then two

years old, smiled when Maj. Gen. Albert F. Hegenberger, former executive officer of the Fourteenth Air Force in China, pinned the Medal of Honor on the
young man's chest. His mother and his grandparents, Mr. and Mrs. Horace S.
Carswell Sr., were by Robert's side during the ceremony. Col. William D. Hop-
son, former commander of the 308th Bomb Group, attended the ceremony,
and troops from nearby military posts and service troops from Goodfellow
Field paraded as the 63rd Army Air Force Band from San Antonio played for
the event.[15]

Carswell was honored in 1948 when Fort Worth Army Air Field was renamed Carswell Air Force Base. The Naval Air Station Joint Reserve Base Fort
Worth now occupies the former air force base, its airstrip called Carswell Field.
There are Carswell Avenues at Elmendorf Air Force Base, Alaska, and Lackland Air Force Base, Texas. The front hall in the Memorial Student Center
at Texas A&M University displays a frame containing an artist's rendition of
Carswell, a specimen medal, and the Medal of Honor citation. After the war
an AMVETS (American Veterans of World War II) post in Fort Worth was
named for him. The Junior Squadron of the Arnold Air Society in the Corps of
Cadets at Texas A&M is named for Carswell. A large bronze bas-relief plaque
of Carswell hangs in the Sam Houston Sanders Corps of Cadets Center on the
campus.

Maj. Horace Seaver Carswell Jr., Class of 1938, was the fourth Texas Aggie
awarded the Medal of Honor. In addition to the Medal of Honor, Carswell was
awarded the Distinguished Service Cross, Distinguished Flying Cross, Purple
Heart, and Air Medal. Without a doubt, he is the most highly decorated Texas
Aggie in school history.

TURNEY WHITE LEONARD
CLASS OF 1942

"He was the bravest man I have ever known."

CAPT. MARION PUGH

TURNEY WHITE LEONARD was born on June 18, 1921, the youngest of six children. His parents were Ernest E. and Lily V. Bell Leonard, who lived in northeast Dallas near the downtown area. In Leonard's application for admission to Texas A&M in June 1938, he states that his mother was widowed when he was one year old, and he was taken to live with his grandparents, Tyree L. and Martha H. Bell. This is the first of several mysteries surrounding Turney Leonard's life. The 1920 U.S. Census shows Ernest and Lily Leonard as married and living in Dallas with five children — Martha Roll, Ernest Jr., Tyree B., John W., and Douglas W. Leonard — with sales manager given as the father's occupation. In the 1930 census, Lily is listed as the head of household, living in Dallas, married, and working as a corsetiere. The same census lists Ernest as married and living in Reno, Nevada, with his occupation listed as advertising salesman. With divorce a rarity and socially unacceptable in those days, it appears that Lily and Ernest separated but did not divorce.[1]

Leonard attended Fannin Grade School in Dallas for four years and then moved to the Rio Grande Valley, where he was a student in the Stuart Place School in Harlingen, completing grade school and one year of high school. He became close to his grandfather, who instilled in him a love of nature and a desire to attend college to study agriculture. When his grandfather died, Leonard returned to Dallas and attended Dallas Technical School. His uncle, Tyree Bell Jr., became his mentor and close friend. Bell, who had graduated from Texas A&M in 1913, was a successful businessman and owner of a large construction company in the city. He was active in affairs at Texas A&M and served as president of the Association of Former Students and a member of the Texas A&M Board of Directors.

The transfer to the Dallas School System provided Leonard, who had always been interested in military training, the opportunity to join the Reserve Officers Training Corps (ROTC) program. In his first year he was awarded a scholarship to attend the ROTC Summer Camp at Camp Dallas, located near Mineral Wells. Camp Dallas was a month-long military training camp sponsored by the Dallas School System for high school ROTC cadets from Dallas and Fort Worth. Leonard excelled in high school and was consistently listed on the honor roll. During his senior year, he was promoted to cadet captain, but much to his regret, he had to drop out of ROTC because he was working in the afternoons.[2]

Leonard was able to continue ROTC training after he enrolled in Texas A&M in September 1938 and was assigned to Company C, Infantry in the

Corps of Cadets. His unit was housed in Goodwin Hall, and he became a waiter in Sbisa Hall, the corps dining facility. James B. "Dick" Hervey, Class of 1942, who years later became the executive secretary of the Texas A&M Association of Former Students, was a freshman with Leonard in Company C and remembers him as an outgoing, very bright, hard-working student who participated fully in freshman, corps, and college activities. When the new cadet dormitories were opened for the 1939–40 school year, Leonard joined the newly activated Company I, Infantry, housed in Dormitory 5, and was promoted to corporal. His roommate was Melville Phillips, and they roomed together for their three upperclassman years.

The honor student continued to excel in school, and in his sophomore year he received the Best Drilled Award for his unit. He also continued his student employment as a waiter, though now in Duncan Hall in the new area. Willard "Will" Worley, Class of 1943, attended Fannin Grade School with Leonard but was one grade behind him. One of his fondest memories of his old schoolmate is when a couple of days into Worley's freshman year, he was on his way to the North Gate when he saw Leonard standing in front of the post office selling brooms to freshmen. Worley stopped to talk to his "hometown buddy," and Leonard told him that he needed to buy a broom. He replied that his roommate had a broom, so he did not need one, but Leonard insisted that all freshmen needed a broom. So Worley, feeling the pressure from an upperclassman, bought a broom.[3]

Leonard was the first sergeant of his cadet company his junior year and company commander his senior year. His company won the Best Drilled Unit in the corps his senior year. In a letter written September 28, 1998, Paul Wischkaemper, Class of 1942, Leonard's classmate and a member of Company I, Infantry, recalled: "I thought Turney was an exceptionally good cadet company commander. His leadership style was based, at its foundation, on his love and therefore sincere respect for people. Although we used the term generously, he was no 'lord and master.' His leadership was leadership, not 'forcemanship.' He got people to want to do the right thing, so they did it. That style was not unusual at A&M, but I thought Turney knew well how to practice it." He later wrote: "As we got into the 1941–42 year, Turney heard about the tank destroyers which General Bruce was beginning to get off the ground. My speculation is that Uncle Tyree Bell '13 and General Bruce '16 were well acquainted because Mr. Bell was so active in alumni affairs. But Turney learned about the tank destroyers before anyone else had heard of them there at A&M and started telling us about it. It all sounded appealing to me because of the mechanized seek, strike, and destroy nature of the mission, as it did to Turney. So he applied for that and was taken in when he graduated." Homer O. Gainer, Class of 1943, remembers Leonard as a studious, industrious, and conscientious student whom his classmates believed was destined for greatness. He earned Distinguished Student status and was a member of the Scholarship Honor Society, Marketing and Finance Club, and the Dallas A&M Club. Leonard graduated on May 16, 1942, with a degree in agricultural administration. Earning honors as a Distinguished Military Graduate, he was commissioned a second lieutenant in the Regular Army, while most of his classmates were commissioned in the U.S. Army Reserve. With the war raging, he and his classmates were desperately needed by the army and were immediately ordered to active duty.[4]

The new officer's first duty assignment was at Camp (later Fort) Hood, where he was a student in the Officer Training Course at the Tank Destroyer Center. The tank-destroyer branch was a new organization formed to provide an increased antitank capability to the army. The commander of the center was Maj. Gen. A. D. Bruce, Class of 1916, who was later known as the "Father of Fort Hood." Bruce was the driving force behind the development of the branch and the fielding of 106 tank-destroyer battalions. After retiring from the army, he became the president and then chancellor of the University of Houston.

Completing the Tank Destroyer Officer Training Course, Leonard was assigned to the center as an instructor. His first contact with the 893rd Tank Destroyer Battalion was at Camp Hood, where the unit was serving as school troops for the brand new Tank Destroyer Tactical and Firing Center.

After a few months as an instructor, he requested transfer to a battalion and was assigned to the 893rd after the unit was transferred to Camp Shelby, Mississippi. Coincidently, his company commander in the battalion was Capt. Marion Pugh, Class of 1941, who was a football legend at Texas A&M and famous as the quarterback of the 1939 National Championship team. Pugh and Leonard developed a close friendship during their unit training at Camp Shelby. The lieutenant was transferred to the battalion staff as the assistant S-2 (intelligence) officer before shipping overseas but returned to his company for combat in Europe.[5]

893RD TANK DESTROYER BATTALION

The 93rd Antitank Battalion was redesignated the 893rd Tank Destroyer Battalion on December 15, 1941, at Fort Meade, Maryland. It was one of fifty-two tank-destroyer battalions the U.S. Army activated in December 1941. By 1944 each of these battalions consisted of a headquarters company, three tank-destroyer gun companies of three platoons each, and a reconnaissance company. The gun platoons had a security section and four M10 tank destroyers that mounted a 3-inch antitank weapon, a total of thirty-six destroyers per battalion. Each battalion was authorized thirty-six commissioned officers, two warrant officers, and 636 enlisted men. A lieutenant colonel commanded the battalion, captains commanded the companies, and lieutenants led the platoons. The reconnaissance company had six M8 armored cars and three M20 armored utility cars.[6]

The 893rd was the first command to arrive at the Tank Destroyer Center at Killeen, Texas. Construction on the center had not begun, and the unit established a temporary camp near Gatesville. The battalion served as the functional prototype of the new tank-destroyer units and was the first to be issued the new T-12 halftrack with the 75-mm gun. During 1942 the 893rd continued its development role as school troops at Camp Hood, training new tank-destroyer formations.

In January 1943 the unit moved to their new home station at Camp Shelby and began an intensive training program to include the Louisiana Maneuvers in April and May. While at Shelby, the T-12 halftracks were replaced with the M10 tank destroyer. The battalion's next move was to Camp Kilmer, New Jersey, and on January 9, 1944, it departed the New York Port of Embarkation. After crossing the Atlantic and arriving in Liverpool, England, on January 17, the 893rd moved to a camp at Chudleigh in Devon, where all new equipment for the battalion was awaiting in a huge abandoned rock quarry. In March the unit transferred to Bridgeport in Dorset.[7]

The battalion boarded ships at Southampton soon after D-Day and landed at the Omaha beachhead on July 1. Once ashore, the unit was placed in support of the 2nd Infantry Division and engaged in the fighting in the Normandy hedgerow country. The hedgerows limited mobility until a new secret weapon, the "Rhino" hedgecutter, was welded to the battalion's M10s. This would finally enable the destroyers to maneuver off the roads and cut through the hedgerows, providing immediate fire support to embattled infantrymen. In late August the battalion was attached to the 4th Infantry Division as the Allies broke out of Normandy and moved east toward Paris. As they approached the French capital, the 893rd was placed in support of the French 2nd Armored Division, which was selected as the Allied unit to liberate the city. The 893rd entered Paris with the French but was soon returned to the 4th Division, joining in the combat across the plains of northern France. By September the battalion had reached Belgium and closed on the German border. The 893rd was awarded

M10 tank destroyer of the 893rd Tank Destroyer Battalion in the Huertgen Forest.
Courtesy National Archives

the Belgium Croix de Guerre with Palms for action in that country September 7–13.[8]

On October 29 the battalion was attached to the 28th Infantry Division and participated in the ill-fated and bloody attack in the Huertgen Forest. When the battered 28th was withdrawn from the battle, the 893rd remained in the woodlands. After receiving new equipment and personnel, the battalion was attached to the 8th Division on November 19 and participated in the capture of the German towns Huertgen, Kleinau, Brandenburg, and Bergstein.[9]

On December 11 the battalion was attached to the 78th Infantry Division and took part in the defensive fighting to hold the northern shoulder of the German counteroffensive during the Battle of the Bulge. Company C, 893rd Tank Destroyer Battalion was awarded the Belgian Croix de Guerre with Palms for actions in the Ardennes December 20, 1944–January 26, 1945. Resuming the offensive, the 78th Division and the attached 893rd recaptured the stronghold of Schmidt and the Roer River dams. Company C was attached to the 82nd Airborne Division February 9–19 and again crossed the Kall River valley to recapture Kommerscheidt. After seeing the Huertgen Forest, the commander of the 82nd, Gen. James M. Gavin, observed that it was a battle that should not have been fought.[10]

The battalion was in support of the 78th Division when the Ludendorff Bridge at Remagen was captured, giving the Allies an intact bridge across the Rhine River. Crossing the Rhine, the division, with the support of the 893rd, expanded the bridgehead and then engaged in the fighting to capture the vast Ruhr industrial region, which became known as the Ruhr Pocket. VE-Day found the 893rd at Altendorf, Germany, about twenty miles north of Frankfurt, where they assumed duties as part of the Army of Occupation. The unit returned to the United States on February 1, 1946, and was deactivated. After the war all tank-destroyer units were disbanded, and the branch ceased to exist.[11]

The 893rd Tank Destroyer Battalion was awarded campaign streamers for Normandy, Northern France, Ardennes-Alsace, Central Europe, and the Rhineland. The unit was also awarded the Belgian Croix de Guerre with Palms, and a second Croix de Guerre with Palms was awarded to the battalion's Company C for a separate action.

BATTLE OF THE HUERTGEN FOREST

The battle of the Huertgen Forest was the longest and one of the bloodiest engagements fought by American forces in Europe, but it has been largely overshadowed by the Battle of the Bulge, which began in December 1944. The Huertgen Forest covers an area of over fifty square miles and is actually composed of three separate forests—Roetgen, Wenau, and Konigl—though American soldiers referred to the area after the town of Huertgen, which was one of their objectives. The region forms a rough triangle that begins about five miles south and east of Aachen and extends to Duren on one side and Monschau on the other. Hilly and densely wooded with conifers, except for cleared ground on the ridges where the towns are located, vehicular movement was limited to a few roads and tracks. Poor weather prevailed during the battle, with fog, rain, snow, and cold, cloudy days.

After the breakout from Normandy, Allied forces had raced across France and reached the German border defenses known to the Allies as the Siegfried Line. A formidable defensive position, the Siegfried Line consisted of concrete

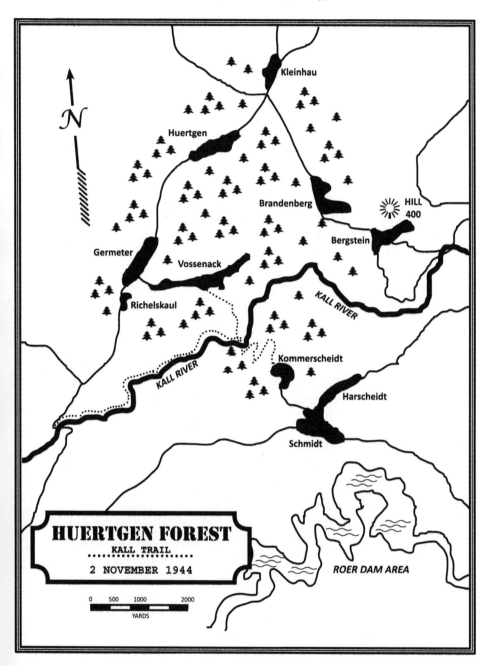

HUERTGEN FOREST

⋯⋯ **KALL TRAIL** ⋯⋯

2 NOVEMBER 1944

0   500   1000   2000

YARDS

bunkers fronted by antitank obstacles. Having outrun their supplies, Allied units paused their offensive here. The U.S. First Army was poised to continue the attack to the Rhine River but was concerned about its right flank along the Huertgen Forest. The U.S. V Corps was ordered to protect this sector by securing the forest. The battle began on September 14, 1944, when a regiment of the 9th Infantry Division attempted to breach the Siegfried Line and capture the Huertgen–Kleinau road network. The attacking unit withdrew after a brief but bloody encounter with German defenders. On October 6 the division again entered the forest, with the crossroads town of Schmidt as their objective. The two attacking regiments pushed some three thousand yards into the forest at a cost of 4,500 casualties.

The battered 9th Division was replaced in late October by the 28th Division, strongly reinforced with tanks, tank destroyers, engineers, and artillery. Rain, mist, fog, and poor visibility postponed a renewal of the attack until November 2. One of the supporting units was the 893rd Tank Destroyer Battalion, which was initially deployed on October 30 to provide indirect-fire support for the division artillery battalions. Company C of the 893rd, commanded by Captain Pugh, was in support of the 112th Infantry Regiment as it made the main effort to seize Schmidt. The attacking infantry jumped off the morning of November 3, and after some minor skirmishes, by nightfall the 3rd Battalion of the 112th controlled the town while the 1st Battalion occupied Kommerscheidt. The Germans responded the next morning with an artillery barrage, followed by an assault with tanks and infantry. The Americans in Schmidt were pushed back to Kommerscheidt, about five hundred yards to the north. Late on the night of November 4, Pugh was ordered to move his company to Kommerscheidt. Early the next morning he learned that the narrow, steep, unimproved track (known as the Kall Trail) that ran through the Kall River valley to Kommerscheidt was blocked by three or four tanks and that engineers and tankers were trying to get the vehicles going or pushed out of the way. The Kall Trail was selected by the 28th Division staff from a map as the main supply route for the division. What appeared to be a road on the map was actually a footpath used by Catholics in Kommerscheidt to walk to Sunday services at the church in Vossenack and had never been used as a road by the Germans.

After the trail was cleared, Pugh moved his force to Kommerscheidt, where he placed Leonard's platoon on the right side of the village and Lt. Goodwin McElroy's platoon on the left side. As Leonard approached the village, he positioned his command in a covered area and went forward on foot to reconnoiter his assigned area. Despite artillery and mortar shells falling in the area, he completed his reconnaissance and led his tank destroyers into the firing positions he had selected. Observing a suspicious haystack and house to his front, he had his guns fire several rounds at these targets. This disclosed his position to an enemy force located in the woods to his rear. The Germans opened fire with an antiaircraft weapon and small arms. Leonard countered by ordering covering fire from his vehicle's 3-inch guns and .50-caliber machine guns. He then moved alone on foot into the woods and discovered the German halftrack that had been firing on his platoon, disabled and ablaze from a round from his destroyers that had also killed several enemy soldiers. Leonard advanced on the burning vehicle and killed the remaining Germans with his submachine gun, eliminating the threat to the platoon's rear.

The following morning, November 5, the enemy in Schmidt attacked Kommerscheidt with infantry and tanks. In order to observe enemy movements better and to provide fire direction to his guns, Leonard took a hand-held radio and left the safety of his command destroyer, his normal station in a firefight, for an open, unobstructed area nearby. Despite heavy shelling and the fire of an enemy machine gun, he remained in his exposed position and continued to direct the fire of his platoon. The resulting accuracy of his tank destroyers knocked out three enemy tanks and helped repel the attack. The lieutenant then advanced on foot in the face of enemy machine-gun fire and personally eliminated the gun and its crew with a hand grenade.

The attack repulsed, Leonard set out on foot to contact U.S. commanders in Kommerscheidt to coordinate plans for a new defense of the area. While moving across the open ground between his position and the infantry command post, he was wounded in the face by a shell fragment. Taken to an aid station, his wounds were treated and bandaged, but he refused to be evacuated. Leonard then proceeded to Kommerscheidt and coordinated his plan of defense with those of the infantry and its supporting tanks from the 707th Tank Battalion.

During the night, Pugh and Lieutenant Fuller of the reconnaissance company left Vossenack in two jeeps with ammunition and rations for Kommerscheidt. Three hundred yards south they ran into about forty German infantrymen. Pugh yelled, "Look out," then opened fire with his jeep's machine gun until it jammed, jumping clear as a rocket hit his windshield. Deflecting a German bayonet lunge with his bare hands, Pugh escaped and made his way back to Vossenack. He was joined there by Fuller, whose jeep had been raked by machine-gun fire. Pugh and Fuller commandeered two of Company B's M10s, returned to the ambush site, and soon dispersed the Germans and foiled their attempt to cut off the Kall Trail. The captain made it through with the supplies, and after distribution he assisted in directing the fire of supporting 8-inch guns to suppress the fire from the high ground around Bergstein.[12]

Just before dawn on the morning of November 6, German infantry attacked the open right flank, where there was no supporting infantry. They came so close that the tank-destroyer crews had to engage in hand-to-hand combat. The assault was repelled, with three additional enemy tanks destroyed and thirty-five to forty enemy infantrymen either killed or wounded. Leonard was constantly on the move during this action, calmly directing fire and providing encouragement to his men.

The American positions in Kommerscheidt came under exceptionally heavy artillery, mortar, and small-arms fire. Disorganized groups of infantry without their leaders, who had been killed or wounded, began to drift to the rear, leaving gaping holes in the defense. Despite the fact that the enemy was close to overrunning the position, Leonard gathered up groups of leaderless infantrymen in his sector and repositioned them to continue fighting, encouraging them despite the seemingly overwhelming enemy superiority. From his exposed position, he directed the fire of his tank destroyers and the supporting tanks to knock out three more enemy tanks. Despite repeated attempts to overrun the position, the Americans held firm. Late during the action, a hit from a high-explosive shell, directed at Leonard's observation post by an enemy tank, wounded him. Shell fragments practically tore off his left arm and wounded him in his legs. Keeping his wits, the lieutenant applied a tourniquet using his belt and walked unassisted in the direction of the aid station. This was the last time the men of his unit saw him. Leonard soon afterward was declared missing in action, and his fate would not be known until 1950, when his body was recovered and identified after years of searching.[13]

Of the nine tank destroyers that Pugh managed to get into Kommerscheidt, seven were knocked out and two were abandoned, and all three of his platoon leaders were killed. The 893rd Tank Destroyer Battalion lost seventeen of its twenty-three tank destroyers available for the action around Vossenack and Kommerscheidt.[14]

The enemy recaptured Kommerscheidt on the afternoon of November 6, 1944, and the area remained in German hands until seized by the 82nd Airborne Division in February 1945. The 28th Division, after suffering more than 6,000 casualties, was replaced on November 19 by the 8th Infantry Division and sent to a quiet sector in the Ardennes to recover. Offensive action in the Huertgen Forest was suspended in December after the Germans began the major counteroffensive in the Ardennes that became known as the Battle of the Bulge. The fighting in the Huertgen Forest had claimed 24,000 Americans killed, wounded, missing, or captured. Another 9,000 soldiers succumbed to trench foot, respiratory diseases, and combat fatigue.[15]

A recommendation for the award of the Medal of Honor to Leonard was submitted by Captain Pugh on January 5, 1945, and was approved by Lieutenant General Hodges, commanding general, First Army, on April 25. When Leonard's mother was contacted about scheduling the presentation of the medal, she requested that the ceremony be held after October 8 so that her three other sons in the service could attend. She added: "There'll be a little more time for Turney, too. I know from what they've told me that he must be dead. Inside, though, I don't feel it. That boy grew up with his grandfather, Tyree L. Bell, in the Rio Grande Valley. He always hunted in the forest, swam in the bayou, and was always out of doors. I haven't grieved for him a bit. I just don't believe there's a German alive that could catch him." Mrs. Leonard was presented the medal by Maj. Gen. Walton H. Walker at Headquarters, 8th Service Command in Dallas on October 24, 1945.[16]

SEARCHING FOR TURNEY LEONARD

The search for Turney Leonard is a story of a mother's love for her son and the hope that he was still alive as a prisoner of war. She insisted that military authorities make every effort to find her son and used political connections to goad the military bureaucracy into action.[17]

Lily Leonard received a telegram on November 27, 1944, reporting her son Turney missing in action. She could not believe he was dead and held out hope that he had been captured. After the war, when there was still no information on the fate of her son, she began a campaign, aided by her brother, Tyree L. Bell, Class of 1913, and Marion Pugh, Class of 1941, to encourage the army to continue the search.

In May 1945 Leonard received a letter from a young French soldier named Jacques Schell. He stated that he had met her son in France, and they became friends. In subsequent letters Schell reported he made several trips to Kommerscheidt to search for Leonard's grave and kept Mrs. Leonard advised of his activities. The Leonard family responded by sending food and clothing to the Schell family. A letter from Schell's mother, Alice Schell, intimated that her son had located two unmarked graves in Kommerscheidt and believed that one might contain the body of his friend.[18]

The army was asked to look into the Schell family. An investigator visited the Schell home at Savigny sur Orge, France, but he obtained no further information to assist in the search and could not confirm the family's claims. Leonard's file contains no additional information about this strange situation, and the Schell family's involvement remains a mystery with many unanswered questions.

In a letter dated May 5, 1947, to the quartermaster general's office (QMG), Bell requested that the army follow up on the lead provided concerning the location of the two graves. Receiving no reply, Bell wrote to the adjutant general of the army expressing his disappointment with the lack of concern by the QMG and the discourtesy in not acknowledging the several inquires made to that office. General Witsell, adjutant general, responded with a letter that was vague and offered assurances that the army was still actively seeking to recover and identify missing personnel. Bell's letter was referred by Witsell to the QMG, which had jurisdiction over the matter.[19]

Bell also wrote to Sen. Tom Connally expressing similar concerns. The senator referred this letter to the QMG on January 10, 1948. The next month the QMG replied that remains recovered from Kommerscheidt believed to be Leonard could not be associated with him for lack of identifying data. The QMG further stated that it had sent letters to former servicemen who might be able to furnish details leading to a recovery.[20]

The previous August, an investigation team visited Kommerscheidt in another effort to find Leonard's remains. In an interview the local burgomaster stated that the residents had been evacuated at the time of the fighting, and upon their return they reported all American remains to the proper German authorities.[21]

Search teams visited Kommerscheidt several times in September and October 1947. A local farmer, Rudolf Lennartz, stated that in April 1945 he had buried most of the deceased soldiers that at the time were laying about the vicinity and had knowledge of the location of American graves. This information proved quite helpful. Bernard Frings, burgomaster of Schmidt and Kommerscheidt in 1945, told investigators that he had remained in Schmidt during the fighting, and after the battle he organized the burial of deceased German and American soldiers. According to his statement, the remains of about fifty U.S. soldiers were disinterred in 1945–46 and evacuated to an American cemetery. To his knowledge there were no more graves in the area. As a result of a thorough search of the Kommerscheidt area and the help of local residents, the search team found the remains of fourteen Americans buried in shell holes, slit trenches, and graves that were marked with German steel helmets.[22]

The QMG's Memorial Division informed Mrs. Leonard that one set of remains recovered at Kommerscheidt might be her son. The tooth chart for the unidentified remains revealed fourteen teeth extracted or missing, while Leonard's dental records showed seven teeth extracted and ten teeth filled. They asked if she was aware of any additional dental work after her son left his last station at Camp Shelby and also requested his shoe size and hair color. Mrs. Leonard responded on July 26, 1948, with the requested information. She also mentioned the wounds he had received to his face in action at Kommerscheidt, of which the identification team apparently was not aware.

The remains in question were designated Unknown X-6667 and were buried at the American Military Cemetery, Neuville-en-Condron, Belgium. A letter dated October 22 from the American Graves Registration Command (AGRC), European Area, to the QMG confirmed that they were not Leonard's remains. Search teams continued to recover and evacuate the remains of American dead, with five bodies recovered in the Kommerscheidt area during November 1947.[23]

As a result of pressure from Senator Connally, the War Department made numerous queries to the AGRC in Europe about the status of the search. Each was answered with a negative report. On November 23, 1948, Congressman Olin E. Teague wrote to the chief of the QMG's Memorial Division requesting a status report on the Leonard case. Again the answer was that extensive searches in the Kommerscheidt area had produced no results. The reply raised the possibility that Leonard's remains might be among those recovered in Kommerscheidt but not identified.

Mrs. Leonard was notified by telegram on November 19, 1949, that her son's status was changed from missing in action to died of wounds on November 7, 1944, with a presumed date of death established as November 8, 1945. The presumed date of death took into consideration its effect on prior military payments and settlements and was in accordance with the policy to establish a date of death one year and one day after being declared missing in action.[24]

Another mystery in the story of Turney Leonard is revealed in a letter his mother sent to the AGRC on October 1, 1949. She wrote that Matthias Bengals, a German national living in Aachen, was searching for her son's grave.

Bengals was formerly with the AGRC, and Mrs. Leonard said she had complete trust and confidence in him. She further stated that he had refused any gifts and was truly interested in finding her son's body. (Again, as with Schell, there is no additional information in the file about Bengals.)[25]

In 1949 several officers of the 112th Infantry Regiment, 28th Division were contacted about the Leonard case and responded with statements about events during the battle at Kommerscheidt. Of the many statements provided, one of the most significant was made by Richard M. Pierce, who was the intelligence officer of the 1st Battalion. On November 7, 1944, he was in a dugout that was being used as a command post in Kommerscheidt. The dugout contained the body of an artillery officer (identified as Capt. Robert C. Driscoll), the wounded Leonard, and three headquarters sergeants. Leonard was placed against one wall in a seated position and administered morphine and a small amount of plasma. The Germans, who had overrun the area, surrounded the dugout and called for the occupants to surrender. After hurriedly discussing the situation with the three sergeants and Leonard, who remained more or less conscious during the entire episode, the Americans surrendered. As they prepared to move Leonard, the lieutenant insisted that they leave him and try to send back German medical aid. The significant point made by Pierce was that Leonard was in a dugout, not an aid station as reported by other battle participants.[26]

The commander of the 112th Infantry Regiment, Lt. Col. Carl L. Peterson, stated that his command post was located in a dugout in an apple orchard in Kommerscheidt and that Driscoll and an unknown tank-destroyer lieutenant, whom he believed to be Leonard, were brought there. He was told after the war that after he left the dugout, a large German tank drove over it.[27]

Maj. Robert T. Haglett, commander of the 1st Battalion, stated that as he was helping drag Driscoll to the dugout, Leonard crawled through a nearby hedgerow asking to be helped to cover. Haglett assisted him into the dugout, noticing that Leonard's left arm was almost completely severed at the shoulder. The lieutenant asked that his Aggie ring on his left hand be placed on his right hand.[28]

A German national, Hubert Dohmen, revealed that during the war he had dug a trench for his family's protection in an apple orchard adjacent to his house in Kommerscheidt. He remembered it measuring about 3.5 meters in length, 2 meters deep, and 2 meters wide and being covered with wooden planks and dirt. When he returned to the village in 1945, he observed that the trench had been used by the Americans and had caved in. Apparently, a tank had driven over it since track marks were left in a nearby hedge. He provided the specific location to a search team.[29]

Maj. R. E. Deppe, Search and Recovery Team 3, AGRC, went to Kommerscheidt on October 27, 1949, to locate the command post pinpointed by Lieutenant Colonel Peterson. Deppe interrogated several local citizens, including Dohmen, and from the information provided was able to locate the site (Dohmen's trench). On October 31 and November 1, his team excavated the area and discovered the body of Leonard, who was in a seated position, his identification tags nearby. After more digging, they discovered Driscoll's remains in a prone position such as a dead man might be. The bodies were recovered and evacuated to the American cemetery in Neuville, Belgium, for positive identification.[30]

Deppe's report of investigation established a partial identification based on the identification tag, statements of former officers of the unit, and Dohmen's statement. The Memorial Division, AGRC, wrote Mrs. Leonard on January 18, 1950, that positive identification had been established for her son. She was informed that his remains had been casketed and were being held in above-ground storage awaiting her instructions. She requested that her son be returned to Dallas for burial.

Leonard's body was shipped from Bremerhaven, Germany, on May 6 aboard the USAT *James E. Robinson* to New York. From there it went by train to Dallas, accompanied by an escort officer, 1st Lt. Charles D. Ellison.[31]

Leonard was eulogized on May 30, 1950, at a ceremony that climaxed Dallas's Memorial Day observance. Services at Crozier Technical High School formally dedicated the American Veterans of World War II Post 22 as the Turney W. Leonard Memorial Post. During an hour-and-a-half program, Gibb Gilchrist, the chancellor of the Texas A&M College System, described Leonard as "a clean young life, dedicated to those things which make for a man—an outstanding scholar—a leader among his fellows—a mark and model to those who follow him."

Marion Pugh paid tribute to his friend and comrade, saying: "Turney Leonard was the bravest and finest person I ever saw or knew. I owe my life to him and there are three hundred others who feel as I do." Congressman Olin E. Teague of the Sixth Congressional District, which includes College Station, said Leonard and others who died gave the nation the time it needed "to work out the salvation of the civilization we know."

The following day Leonard found his final resting place at Grove Hill Memorial Park in Dallas. Funeral services were conducted by Rev. Homer R. Reynolds, pastor of the Ross Avenue Baptist Church and chaplain of the Reserve 443rd Troop Carrier Wing, Hensley Field. Pallbearers were Pugh and classmates from the Class of 1942, J. B. "Dick" Hervey, George Adams, Rod D. Gambrell Jr., Vincent DePaul Hagan, and Fred Smithham.[32]

RETURN OF THE AGGIE RING

The Aggie ring is one of the most cherished items a graduate of Texas A&M University possesses, and most graduates wear their ring for life. Very few institutions other than the military academies, the Citadel, Virginia Military Institute, and perhaps a few other schools have a similar tradition. The original Aggie ring, cast in solid gold, was designed in the late 1880s and featured an intertwined "AMC" surrounded by four diamonds. In 1894 a ring committee was formed to design what has evolved into today's Aggie ring. With only minor changes, the ring has remained essentially the same. The Association of Former Students is responsible for distributing the rings and exercises tight controls on those who are permitted to purchase one.[33]

In 1946 a fifteen-year-old German, Alfred Hutmacher, was employed by an American team searching for war dead in the Kommerscheidt area. While digging in the area of a suspected burial, he found a large gold ring and put it in his pocket. He had no idea what it signified, and when he returned home he put it in a box in his bureau drawer. There it remained, forgotten for over fifty years, until his son-in-law, Volker Lossner, an officer in the German army, expressed interest in the battle in the Huertgen Forest. A few days later Hutmacher recalled finding the ring and showed it to Lossner. At the time the officer did not understand the significance of the ring either, but after finding a name engraved inside, he knew it might be important to someone. He and his father-in-law agreed to try to return it to the family if they could be located. Lossner visited the U.S. Army Liaison Office in Bonn and showed the ring to Col. Thomas Fosnacht, who identified it as a class ring from Texas A&M. The engraved name meant nothing to him, though, so he searched the Internet for the name Leonard Turney, but had no success. He and Lossner reversed the name and searched for Turney Leonard, adding Kommerscheidt to the search. They were immediately rewarded with information about Leonard and learned that he had received the Medal of Honor for actions at Kommerscheidt. Fosnacht now realized the importance of the ring and told Lossner that he would try to contact someone at Texas A&M.

On October 17, 2000, at an Association of the U.S. Army conference in Washington, D.C., Fosnacht mentioned the ring to retired general Trent

Douglas Leonard and German army lieutenant Volker Lossner at the ceremony in
the Corps of Cadets Center marking the return of Turney Leonard's Aggie ring on
November 11, 2000. Courtesy Cushing Memorial Library and Archives,
Texas A&M University

Thomas and told him about the desire of Lossner and Hutmacher to return the
ring to Leonard's relatives. The next day Thomas sent an e-mail to his friend,
Howard Graves, chancellor of the Texas A&M University System at College
Station. Graves called Thomas, heard the story of the ring, and said that the information had been sent to Dr. Ray Bowen, Class of 1958, president of Texas
A&M. Bowen contacted Thomas and said he would like to facilitate the return
of the ring, and hopefully the German officer could be brought to campus to
present the ring personally. The necessary arrangements were made, and a few
days later Lossner's commander asked him if he could travel to College Station
to return the ring. An instructor at the German Army Maintenance School at
the time, Lossner replied that he had several classes he was teaching and could
not leave until the course was completed. Shortly thereafter, he was ordered by
his superiors to be prepared to leave for the United States the following week,

*Display in the Sam Houston Sanders Corps of Cadets Center containing
Turney Leonard's Medal of Honor and Aggie ring.* Courtesy Sam Houston Sanders
Corps of Cadets Center, Texas A&M University

accompanied by Fosnacht and a German colonel. Travel arrangements were
courtesy of the university, and when the party arrived in College Station, they
were warmly received by the Aggie community.

In a ceremony at the Sanders Corps of Cadets Center on November 11,
2000, Lossner said, "I have come a long way to honor a brave son of this country and graduate of this university—a man who brought honor to his nation, to
his fellow countrymen, to his school, and to his name." He then presented the
ring to Turney Leonard's brother Douglas, who represented the thirty family
members present. Holding the ring high, the elder Leonard stated, "This will
not leave A&M College," and then called his nephew, Tyree Bell Leonard, Class
of 1965, to come forward with Leonard's Medal of Honor, which he presented
to President Bowen. Following the ceremonies, the Leonard family and Loss-

ner's party attended the A&M-Oklahoma football game at Kyle Field and were recognized on the field at halftime.[34]

A display case in the Corps Center contains Leonard's class ring and Medal of Honor, along with pictures and memorabilia from his cadet days at Texas A&M and his service with the 893rd Tank Destroyer Battalion. Above the display case hangs a large bronze bas-relief plaque of Leonard.

The circumstances surrounding the loss and return of the ring presents another mystery in the life of Turney Leonard. Sitting in the dugout after being seriously wounded, he had asked Major Haglett to remove his ring from his left hand and place it on his other hand. This may have been done, or perhaps the ring was just placed in Leonard's right hand. Shortly after this, the dugout was surrounded by the enemy and the occupants surrendered, leaving Leonard inside to await medical aid. Realizing that he was about to be taken prisoner, perhaps he threw his ring away or pushed it into the earthen wall of the dugout to prevent the Germans from taking it.

LEONARD HONORS

In addition to the display of the ring and Medal of Honor in the Corps Center, Texas A&M University has honored Leonard in other ways. In 1969 Dormitory 7 was renamed Turney W. Leonard Hall. A framed display containing an artist's rendition of Leonard, a specimen Medal of Honor, and the citation for the medal hangs in the front hall of the Memorial Student Center. After the war AMVETS Post 22 in Dallas was named in his honor. And Leonard's exploits in the Huertgen Forest have been recounted in several books about the battle.

First Lt. Turney White Leonard, Class of 1942, was the fifth Texas Aggie to be awarded the Medal of Honor.

ELI LAMAR WHITELEY

CLASS OF 1941

"Don't die for your country; let the other sonofabitch die for his."

GEN. GEORGE S. PATTON

THE WHITELEY FAMILY FARM was located on the banks of the North San Gabriel River in an area called Hunt Hollow, named after the family of Eli Lamar Whiteley's mother. It was a typical Texas Hill Country farm, with a thin layer of top soil, hilly terrain, and an abundance of live oaks, cedars, mesquite, and prickly pear cactus; more suited for goats than for crops. The main products of the Whiteley farm were Angora goats, turkeys, and some crops, mostly cotton and grains, grown in the bottomlands along the river. The nearest town was Liberty Hill on the eastern fringe of the Hill Country and about twelve miles west of Georgetown.

Eli Lamar Whiteley was born on December 10, 1913, the son of Eli Whiteley and Ruth Hunt Whiteley. His older brother, Thaddeus E. Whiteley, was born on January 14, 1911. He and his brother grew up on the farm helping their father with the livestock and crops. When six years old, Whiteley started grammar school at Bell School. The country school had a "low" first and a "high" first, so he spent two years in the first grade. When the family moved to Georgetown, the boy enrolled in the Georgetown Public School System and completed his elementary education in 1927. He participated in school activities, and in the eighth grade he served as chairman of the program committee that planned parties and picnics for the class.

In the fall of 1927, Whiteley enrolled in Georgetown High School. As a sophomore he participated in a prank on the night before Senior Day, when a group of juniors and sophomores captured the seniors, took them into the country, and left them to walk back to town. He was active in the Future Farmers of America (FFA) and a member of the FFA livestock-judging team. When the club took a trip to Galveston, Huntsville, and Houston during the summer of 1928, he was in charge of planning and financing the trip. He was also the camp boss and chief cook.

While in high school, he was active in sports, playing football for two years and running track for three. He was also interested in public speaking and debating and was a member of the Debate Club. During the last half of his senior year, the family moved to Andice, a small town near Florence. Whiteley wanted to graduate with his class and elected to remain in Georgetown. He found a job on a dairy farm working for his room and board; it was hard work and the hours were long. Because of his duties at the dairy, he was disappointed when he had to miss the activities of his Senior Day, but he was able to graduate with his class on May 21, 1932.

Whiteley applied for admission to Texas A&M during the summer of 1932, stating that he wanted to study civil engineering. He also planned to work his

way through school. In August 1932 the assistant registrar wrote his father rec-
ommending that his son do additional work in high school or at a junior college. If admitted to A&M, however, he would be on probation with the understanding that if his work was not satisfactory, he would be dropped from the
rolls. This probably resulted from selecting engineering as his course of study
due to his weak record in mathematics. Whiteley decided that he would not
enroll in college at that time but would work and save enough to pay for his
education. The effects of the Great Depression were being felt in Central Texas
by this time, and it was not easy to save money. He worked on local ranches,
at a service station, in a tailor shop, as a waiter, and even built rock fences and
chopped cedar. After three years doing odd jobs, Whiteley found employment
with the Agricultural Adjustment Administration (AAA), staying on for three
years. The AAA administrated a program to raise the value of crops by paying
farmers subsidies for leaving some of their fields unused, thus reducing agricultural surpluses.

One year turned into two, and before long Whiteley had spent six years
of hard work saving for college. It was not until 1938 that he reapplied to
A&M. He was admitted, but this time he selected agriculture as his course of
study, stating that he wanted to work for the extension service after graduation. Whiteley selected the cavalry branch for his required military science and
was assigned to Headquarters Troop, Cavalry in the Corps of Cadets. He arrived in College Station with $125.25, and the first day A&M took $80 for tu-
ition, books, and uniforms. During his time in college, Whiteley continued to
work to pay for his college expenses. He worked two jobs, one at the Humpty
Dumpty grocery store in downtown Bryan and the other in a local café. He
also did odd jobs like waxing the floors of some of the finest homes in Bryan.
Entering college at age twenty-four, he was not the traditional freshman but
was determined to make up for lost time and graduate as soon as possible. He
took a heavy academic load and attended summer school for three years, at the
end of which he was academically classified a senior. Whiteley graduated with a
bachelor of science in agriculture on August 30, 1941. Graduating in three years
did not permit him to receive a military contract that would lead to an officer's
commission since he could not complete the required ROTC courses in that
time.[1]

After graduating, Whiteley went to Raleigh, North Carolina, to attend
graduate school at North Carolina State College. When America entered the
war on December 7, 1941, he knew that he would be needed sooner or later,
so he wrote Travis Bryan, chairman of the Brazos County Draft Board, to put

his name on the next call. He was drafted into the army on April 12, 1942, and sent to Camp Wolters, Texas, for basic training. After completion, Whiteley was selected to attend a three-week noncommissioned officers school, graduating on September 19. He was then accepted for officers training at the Infantry Officers Candidate School, Class 169, at Fort Benning, Georgia. On February 10, 1943, he was discharged with the rank of corporal, after serving nine months and twenty-seven days as an enlisted man, to accept a commission as a second lieutenant. Returning to Camp Wolters ten days later, he was assigned to the Infantry Replacement Training Center as a training officer. In April 1944 he was ordered again to Fort Benning, Georgia, to attend the Infantry Officers Advanced Course. After graduation he returned to Camp Wolters to continue duties as a training officer.

Whiteley received orders for Europe and shipped out on November 10, arriving in England a week later. He departed England on November 18 and landed in France the following day. Assigned to the 15th Infantry Regiment, 3rd Infantry Division, he joined Company L as a rifle-platoon leader. At the time the 15th was engaged in the fighting at Epinal in the Vosges Mountains of Alsace in eastern France.[2]

15TH INFANTRY REGIMENT

The 15th U.S. Infantry Regiment was constituted on May 3, 1861, at Newport Barracks, Kentucky. Before the end of the Civil War, the regiment had fought twenty-two major engagements, including Chattanooga, Chickamauga, Murfreesboro, and Atlanta. Afterward the 15th served on occupation duty in Alabama until 1869. The regiment then was deployed to the West, serving in Missouri, New Mexico, Dakota Territory, and Colorado. It participated in campaigns against the Ute Indians of Colorado and Utah and the Mescalero Apaches in New Mexico and Arizona before relocating to Fort Sheridan, Wyoming, in January 1891.

At the outbreak of the Spanish-American War in 1898, the regiment moved to Huntsville, Alabama, for intensive training. It shipped from Savannah, Georgia, in November for Nuevitas, Cuba, and occupation duties following the close of hostilities. On October 5, 1899, the regiment returned to the United States and was stationed at several small posts in upper New York and Vermont.

The 15th Infantry was transferred to China in August 1900, arriving in Tientsin to perform security duties as part of the China Relief Expedition in the aftermath of the Boxer Rebellion. The next month 3rd Battalion was ordered to Manila to assist in suppressing the Philippine Insurrection. By April 1902 the balance of the regiment joined the 3rd Battalion in the Philippines and saw considerable action against rebels on Luzon.

In September the regiment was relieved and sailed for Monterey, California. While stationed at Monterey, members of the regiment doubled as engineers and built much of the Presidio of Monterey. In 1905 the regiment returned to the Philippine Islands and saw minimal action against the few remaining rebels. After two years overseas, the regiment returned to the United States, assigned to garrison duty at Fort Douglas, Utah.

The 2nd Battalion, 15th Infantry departed for China in November 1911 to join the international peacekeeping forces assigned to protect American and other foreign interests there. The 3rd Battalion followed in early 1912, while the 1st Battalion was retained in the Philippines. During the interminable revolutions, rebellions, and civil wars in China, the battalions performed the mission of protecting Tientsin from marauding bandits and disaffected soldiers. Much of the 15th Infantry's regimental traditions and its motto derive from the twenty-six years in China. The dragon on the shield of the regimental coat of arms and Pidgin English motto "Can Do" epitomize this influence.

The regiment was relieved from its duty in China in March 1938 and departed for Fort Lewis, Washington. In January 1939 the 15th Infantry was assigned to the 3rd Infantry Division. For the next two years, the regiment trained as the army's only experimental ski unit and also received training in amphibious assault landings along the Pacific Coast.

After Pearl Harbor the 15th served as part of the security for the northwest United States until October 1942, when it moved to Virginia and prepared for deployment to Europe. On November 8 the 15th landed at Fedela, Morocco, and participated in the capture of Casablanca against strong Vichy French resistance. The regiment remained in Morocco until March 1943, when it moved to Tunisia to train for the invasion of Sicily. In July 1943 the 15th landed in Sicily and fought with distinction at Palermo, Messina, and elsewhere.

In January 1944 the 15th spearheaded the 3rd Infantry Division's landing at Anzio and participated in the capture of Rome. On August 15 the regiment led the landings in southern France. It also led the divisional attacks through the Rhone valley and conducted the first military crossing of the Vosges Mountains. Reaching the Rhine River on November 26, from December 1944 to February 1945 its men fought to reduce the Colmar Pocket. The regiment was part of the 3rd Division's advance into Germany, capturing Nuremberg in April 1945. After the war the 15th Infantry remained in Germany on occupation duty until September 1946, when it deployed to Fort Benning, Georgia. By the end of World War II, the regiment had sixteen Medal of Honor recipients and had suffered losses of 1,633 killed, 5,812 wounded, and 419 missing in action.

In 1950 the regiment was ordered to Korea and first saw action in North Korea, where it helped protect the withdrawal of the 1st Marine Division from the Chosin Reservoir. For the next two years, the regiment fought in Korea, remaining there until 1954, when it returned to Fort Benning. In 1957 the 15th Infantry, now reorganized into two battle groups, was assigned to Germany. With the reorganization of the army in the 1960s, the regimental organization as known in World War II and Korea ceased to exist. Regimental traditions were passed to the battalions that carried the colors of the associated regiment.

During its illustrious history, the 15th Infantry Regiment earned five Presidential Unit Citations, a Navy Unit Commendation, two French Croix de Guerre, two Republic of Korea Presidential Unit Citations, and the Gold Bravery Medal of Greece.[3]

BATTLE OF SIGOLSHEIM
For the 15th Infantry Regiment, the road to Sigolsheim, France, began on August 15, 1944, when Allied forces conducted a three-division assault on the beaches of southern France. The 3rd Infantry Division came ashore on the left at Cavalaire-sur-Mer (its fourth major landing against a hostile shore), the 45th Infantry Division landed in the center at Saint-Tropez, and the 36th Infantry Division landed on the right at Saint-Raphael. French commando forces landed on both flanks of the main invasion force while U.S. and British airborne troops dropped inland.

The landing forces met light resistance and were soon advancing north up the Rhone River valley. By August 23 the enemy's Nineteenth Army was almost completely disorganized because of the speed and success of the Allied advance assisted by the activity of French resistance groups. After the capture of Montelimar on August 29, the 3rd Division turned northeast in its race to Besancon, a key communications and road center near the Swiss border. After heavy fighting, the town fell to the Americans on September 9.[4]

The division continued to push north against heavy resistance, arriving at the approaches to the Vosges Mountains. Although it was still mid-Autumn, cold winds had begun to blow already, and the weather had turned rainy. The granite massif of the Vosges rises steeply from the Plains of Alsace, lies northeast–southwest, and blocks easy entrance to the Rhine valley from the west. The Vosges consist of low, generally rounded mountains from 1,000 to 4,000 feet

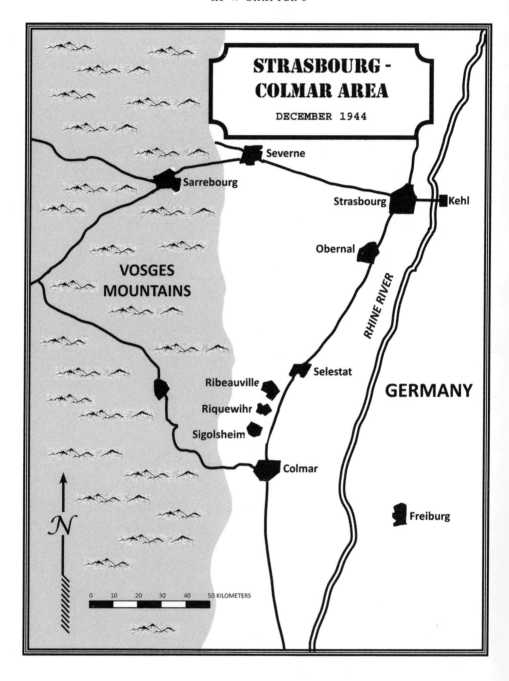

STRASBOURG - COLMAR AREA

DECEMBER 1944

Severne

Sarrebourg

Strasbourg

Kehl

Obernal

RHINE RIVER

VOSGES MOUNTAINS

Ribeauville

Riquewihr

Sigolsheim

Selestat

GERMANY

Colmar

Freiburg

N

0 10 20 30 40 50 KILOMETERS

in height, arranged in parallel ridges. The area is heavily forested, and the road net is somewhat restricted by the terrain.[5]

From September 22 to November 28, against strong opposition, the division fought through many small towns and villages, crossed the Moselette and Meutrhas rivers, and reached the vicinity of Strasbourg, which had been captured by French forces. The division took up defensive positions along the Rhine River south of Strasbourg on the edge of the Plains of Alsace. Enemy forces west of the river were frustrated in their efforts to hold a sizable salient, known as the "Colmar Pocket," when elements of the French First Army reached the Rhine just above Basel, Switzerland.[6]

On December 17 the 3rd Division moved south to relieve the battered 36th Division, taking over defensive positions facing German forces in the Colmar Pocket. The salient, on the west bank of the Rhine, covered an area forty miles long and thirty miles deep. On the twenty-third the 15th Infantry launched an attack against the towns of Bennwihr and Sigolsheim as the first step in securing a more stable line of defense. The towns were located at the extreme western edge of Alsatian plain and just east of the last high slopes of the Vosges. Advance reconnaissance indicated that Sigolsheim in particular was strongly occupied by the enemy.

At H-hour, 7:30 AM, the 1st Battalion's Companies A and C attacked Sigolsheim against stiff resistance and reached the edge of the town at noon. The small village was a shambles, having been reduced by bombers, artillery, and tank fire. Meanwhile, the 3rd Battalion attacked Bennwihr from the north and west. Under the cover of darkness, Companies K and L (Whiteley's unit) struck Bennwihr again in an early morning thrust, this time from the east. Moving in, the infantrymen commenced the dangerous, physically exhausting work of eliminating the enemy from the rubble of houses and cellars. By early afternoon a major portion of the town had been cleared. Having entered the battle with 125 men, at the conclusion of the fighting, Company L was down to 56 men. Whiteley's platoon dropped from 36 men to 8.[7]

In Sigolsheim several armored vehicles supporting the 1st Battalion bogged down in the muddy terrain, thus reducing the striking power of the attack. The battalion was still attempting to gain a good toehold when the enemy counterattacked with infantry and armor late that night. Coming under mortar and artillery fire from Hill 351 to the north, the unit's position became untenable. The battalion relinquished its slender hold and withdrew to Kientzheim and Riquewihr for the night. It was now apparent that before any position in Sigolsheim could be held, the enemy must be driven from Hill 351. On the morning of December 24, the 1st Battalion attacked up the northwestern slope of the hill from the direction of Riquewihr. Company A reached the top of the hill twice but was forced to withdraw. Companies B and C succeeded in reaching the northeast slopes of the hill by noon. At this point the battalion commander, Lt. Col. Keith L. Ware, led a handful of men and a tank in a daring assault of the enemy positions on top of 351. At the end of this assault, 20 German dead were counted, 30 were captured, and about 150 crack SS troops were put to flight. Ware was awarded the Medal of Honor for this action. (As a major general, he became the highest-ranking officer to die in Vietnam when his helicopter crashed.)

Companies K and L attacked the east side of Sigolsheim on Christmas night but were driven back. The town was now the sole remaining objective of the regiment's offensive. It was attacked again on December 26, with Company K advancing along the north road into town, Company L moving along the center road, and Company G taking the south road. The enemy put up a desperate defense as they fell back from house to house.[8]

During Company L's bitter fight to clear out Sigolsheim, 1st Lt. Eli L. Whiteley particularly distinguished himself. His story is best told by the eyewitness accounts of two members of his platoon. Pfc. John R. Sheeley of Pomario, South Carolina, stated in his account of the battle:

> Lieutenant Whiteley charged ahead and headed for a house where enemy [soldiers] were firing. There was an artillery burst near him and he was wounded. I saw that he had been hit in the arm and elbow and his shirt was torn. He was carrying a submachine gun and he rushed the house and there was a rattle of firing inside. When I got in I saw two dead Germans and Lieutenant Whiteley was tearing feathers out of a pillow. He hung the pillow, loaded with grenades, around his wounded shoulder and started down the street into the German fire. He advanced by throwing fragmentation and smoke grenades in front of him and then went through the smoke. He used a fragmentation grenade to blast the door down of the next place off its hinges and then charged inside. When I went in behind him I saw him shoot a Kraut through the head as the German fired on him. I saw another sprawled on the floor with a machine pistol in his hand and 11 others were against a wall, begging him not to kill them. When we got down the street to the last house there was a lot of fire. The Krauts were dropping mortar shells into the street and had everything covered with automatic fire. We had too many wounded to take on what looked like a suicide job. Lieuten-

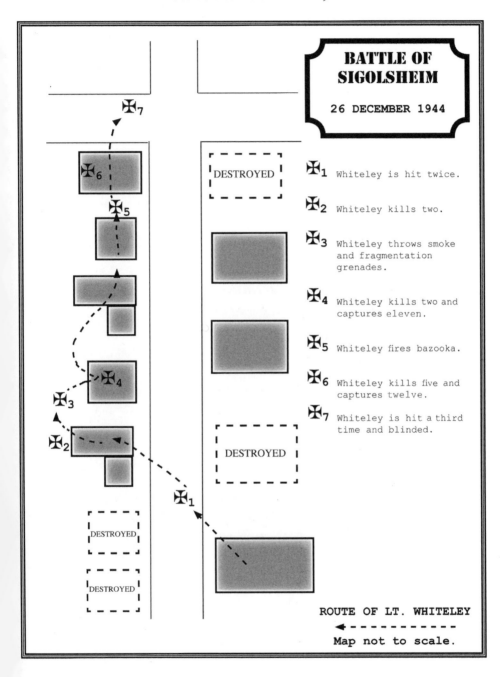

BATTLE OF SIGOLSHEIM

26 DECEMBER 1944

1 Whiteley is hit twice.

2 Whiteley kills two.

3 Whiteley throws smoke and fragmentation grenades.

4 Whiteley kills two and captures eleven.

5 Whiteley fires bazooka.

6 Whiteley kills five and captures twelve.

7 Whiteley is hit a third time and blinded.

ROUTE OF LT. WHITELEY

◄ - - - - - - - - - - -

Map not to scale.

ant Whiteley took a bazooka and, with another man holding it, moved into
the street and tore out the whole wall of the house with his first shot. He
went through the hole in the wall and killed five Germans who had been in
the front room. And bullets from his submachine gun tore through the wall,
and 12 scared Germans in a back room came out to surrender.

The second eyewitness was Pfc. Charles K. Donaldson of Mars, Pennsylvania,
who wrote:

> When the lieutenant came out of the last place and was wounded by the
> burst we all knew he was badly hurt. His face was convulsed with pain, but
> he still wanted to go forward. He couldn't see, I could tell by the way he
> stumbled and weaved. He was trying to keep the fact that he was blinded
> from the men. We begged him to go back for aid. He was very seriously
> wounded. But he refused and when our company commander, Lieutenant
> Wann, asked him to go back he insisted on leading the fight. The only way
> Lieutenant Wann could make him go back was to knock him out cold. You
> couldn't stop our men after that.

Late that night, the town was cleared of the enemy, and the 15th Infantry had
captured another one hundred prisoners. Whiteley was credited with killing
nine Germans, capturing twenty-three others, and spearheading the attack that
cracked the core of enemy resistance in Sigolsheim. He was awarded the Medal
of Honor for his actions.[9]

Hours after the battle, Whiteley was taken to the aid station, which was
overwhelmed with casualties. He had suffered head, arm, shoulder, and leg
wounds and was covered in blood. A doctor took one look at him, shook his
head, and walked away. Sometime later a French doctor assisting the Americans noticed Whiteley lying by the aid station and went to examine him.
The Frenchman realized that he was still alive and began to treat his massive
wounds. For Whiteley, his military war was over, but another war had begun.
His first battle was to live, then several more to recover from his many wounds,
and finally to return to a normal civilian life. The road was a long one. On
December 27 he was moved from the battalion aid station to the 51st Evacuation Hospital at St. Die, some thirty miles northwest of Sigolsheim. On January 3, 1945, he was at the 21st General Hospital at Mirecourt, about forty miles
west of St. Die. From Mirecourt he was evacuated by hospital train to the 43rd
General Hospital in Avignon in southern France, arriving there on January 20.
He then was returned to the United States, landing on March 7 at Charleston,

Pres. Harry S. Truman presents the Medal of Honor to Capt. Eli L. Whiteley at the White House on August 23, 1945. Courtesy National Archives

South Carolina, where he was admitted to the Stark General Hospital. After a cross-country trip on a hospital train, he arrived at Dibble Army Hospital in Menlo Park, California. Dibble specialized in plastic surgery, blind care, neuro-psychiatry, and orthopedics. Whiteley spent eighteen months in and out of the hospital, undergoing plastic surgery. He was fitted with an artificial eye during this period.

With plenty of time between surgeries and treatments, he took up the game of bridge, spending many hours with fellow patients perfecting his game. He became an accomplished player and continued to play frequently after his return to civilian life. He also filled some of his downtime at the hospital as a part-time employee at the nearby Menlo Park Racetrack.

While a patient in California, Whiteley was summoned to the White House for a ceremony on August 23, 1945, for the presentation of his Medal of Honor. His mother, father, and brother were also invited to witness Pres. Harry Truman present the medal. Whiteley traveled to Washington, D.C., by train with an officer escort. His mother also made the train trip to the capital, but his father could not attend because he could not leave his farm unattended. His brother Thaddeus, who was en route to an army assignment in the Philippines, was ordered to Washington to attend the ceremony.

Afterward Whiteley returned to Dibble for more treatment and was finally discharged on May 21, 1946. He had been promoted to captain on March 23. Whiteley returned to the Texas A&M campus in April for the Aggie Muster, where the Aggie Medal of Honor recipients were honored. The muster was held at Kyle Field, and the speaker was General of the Army Dwight D. Eisenhower.[10]

LIFE AFTER THE WAR

Whiteley returned to Texas A&M after his discharge and was a lecturer in freshman agronomy classes. He reapplied for admission to North Carolina State College to complete his graduate studies and was admitted with the offer of an assistantship. While a graduate student, through a mutual friend, he met Anna Morris Saunders of Laurenberg, North Carolina. She was a student at Peace College, a small liberal-arts college for women in Raleigh. They dated for several months until Whiteley received his master's degree in September 1949 and returned to Texas, where he accepted an offer of a teaching position in the Agronomy Department at Texas A&M. After returning to Texas, he called Saunders and proposed marriage. She accepted the offer and agreed to come to Texas for the marriage—but told her sister that if she did not like "those people," she was coming home. Apparently, she liked "those people" because the marriage took place on September 11, 1949, at the home of Thaddeus Whiteley in Sulphur Springs, Texas. A honeymoon was planned in Galveston, but the couple got only as far as College Station.

Whiteley and his bride settled down in the college town, buying a house a few blocks east of campus. Their first child, Eli Lamar Jr., was born in 1950, followed by daughters Ruth Lynn in 1953, Alice Susan in 1955, Mary Elizabeth in 1958, and another son, Macon Morris, in 1962. Their big backyard was devoted to a vegetable garden, and with Whiteley's knowledge of soils and crops, enough was produced to feed the family and neighbors.[11]

Whiteley was granted full admission to the doctoral program at A&M in February 1954 and earned his Ph.D. on January 17, 1959, with the dissertation, "An Investigation of Some of the Effects of Anhydrous Ammonia on the Clay Minerals, Montmorillonite and Illite."[12]

While working on his doctorate, Whiteley taught classes in agronomy and was engaged in research. In 1961 he was assigned to full-time research on new crops. His work involved soybeans, narrow-row cotton, canola, fennel, kenaf, sugar beets, and hops. He had research projects all over the state in such places as Lubbock, Corpus Christi, Thrall, Splendora, Prairie View, and Kenner as well as the university farms in the Brazos valley. Whiteley spent many days traveling to check the progress of his research crops. He had an office and laboratory in the basement of the agronomy building that contained a machine shop in which he developed the equipment needed in his work. When fellow researchers had equipment problems, they could count on help from Whiteley, who also repaired the equipment used in his own research.

His office had a large table that served as a meeting place for morning coffee with fellow faculty members and for bridge games during the noon hour. Everyone understood that the stool at the head of the table was reserved for Dr. Whiteley, and it was an ongoing joke among the department staff, faculty, and graduate students that they would not tell newcomers of this arrangement. One new graduate student, Murray Milford, learned the hard way, for while sitting on the stool at the head of the table, Whiteley came in and popped him on the head with his Aggie ring. All present had a good laugh. Milford later joined the department and was associated with Whiteley for many years. He remembers Whiteley as a man who had an unassuming personality and was highly respected by students, staff, and faculty.[13]

Gene Bolton of Franklin, Texas, started working for Whiteley in 1957 as a laboratory technician. He also worked for Drs. Morris Bloodworth and

George Knuze until 1961, when he was assigned to assist Whiteley full time in research on new crops. Bolton remembers his boss as being loyal to his friends and a hard worker who was not afraid to get his hands dirty. Bolton worked for Whiteley for twenty-six years and has the highest praise for him as an employer and a person.[14]

After retiring from the university, Whiteley continued to work as a consultant. One project took him to Arizona as he continued to push for kenaf as an alternative for paper production. Some of his consulting work was for his former students, who still sought his expertise and advice.

Serving as president of the Congressional Medal of Honor Society, Whiteley traveled extensively to represent the organization. He also served as the commander of the local American Legion post. Inducted into the Infantry School Hall of Fame at Fort Benning, Georgia, he was also a member of many organizations, including Sigma Xi, Phi Kappa Phi, American Society of Agronomy, and the Soil Science Society of America. His honors included listings in *Who's Who in the South and Southwest, Personalities of the South,* and *American Men and Women of Science.*[15]

Whiteley was selected to speak at the 1962 Aggie Muster on the A&M campus. The muster was held in the Memorial Student Center since it was Easter weekend and very few students were on campus. Because only a few people actually heard the speech, the full text was published in the student newspaper, *The Battalion,* on April 26 and could be read in its entirety by absent administration staff, faculty, and students. It was a tumultuous time for the college. Several committees were submitting plans and recommendations for the future of the institution. The most contentious proposals concerned the admission of women and the status of the Corps of Cadets. "Traditionalists" wanted to maintain A&M as an all-male military college, while the committees recommended a change to a coeducational college without the military-science requirement.

Whiteley's speech included four points directed at former students. After covering the first three, he came to his final position: "Fourth, and this, I think, is the most important part of our role as ex-students, we need to support the decision of the administrative officers. Changes that are made by the Board of Directors, the chancellor, the president, and the deans of the colleges are to be accepted. Changes have always been made in the policies under which A&M has operated." This was a brave and unpopular stance for a former student to take.[16]

The veteran often told his family that he would like to return to the Sigol-

Eli Whiteley lies in state in the rotunda of the Systems Administration Building on the campus of Texas A&M University as members of the Ross Volunteer Company stand vigil. Courtesy Cushing Memorial Library and Archives, Texas A&M University

sheim and Colmar area for a visit. He had the opportunity in November 1986, when he was invited by the citizens of Bennwihr, France, to attend their Liberation Day celebration. Whiteley was accompanied by his wife, daughter Ruth, and sister-in-law Alice Prevatt. While in France they visited Sigolsheim and also took the opportunity to tour the Vosges Mountains and the Colmar area.[17]

HONORS FOR A HERO

Eli Lamar Whiteley died at the age of seventy-two of a heart attack on December 2, 1986. His flagged-draped coffin was placed in the rotunda of the Systems Administration Building, and members of the Ross Volunteers stood vigil as university administrators, faculty, students, friends, and family came to pay tribute. Whiteley became only the second person to lie in state on the campus of Texas A&M, the first being Earl Rudder, who died in office while president of the university.

Military cortege with a World War I–style wagon carrying Eli Whiteley's flag-draped coffin, accompanied by an honor guard and riderless horse, passes through the Texas A&M campus. Courtesy Cushing Memorial Library and Archives, Texas A&M University

The funeral service was held in Rudder Theater, with Rev. Bruce Fisher, pastor of the A&M Presbyterian Church, presiding. Fisher told the crowd of family, friends, and admirers that had mustered for the funeral, "We are gathered at this time to honor a true American hero." Jerry Gaston, A&M associate provost, paid further tribute to Whiteley: "Texas A&M University has lost a friend, a loyal former student, a dedicated professor, and the only survivor of the distinguished group of Texas A&M Congressional Medal of Honor winners."

Afterward the casket was carried from the theater by an honor guard from Fort Hood and placed on a World War I–style artillery wagon, marking the beginning of a military-honors funeral procession. With members of the Corps of Cadets lining each side of the street, a riderless horse and members of Parson's Mounted Cavalry led the military cortege as it wound its way across campus to the East Gate, where the coffin was placed in a hearse for transport to College

Station City Cemetery. The burial was with full military honors, and the folded American flag was presented to the family. Included among the many guests at the funeral were four Medal of Honor recipients.[18]

He was honored by Texas A&M when a dormitory was renamed Eli L. Whiteley Hall. Additionally, the university dedicated a memorial park on the west side of the campus to him. A large bronze-bas relief plaque hangs in the Sanders Corps of Cadets Center. Below the plaque is a display case containing Whiteley's Medal of Honor, cadet and military insignia, photos, division patch, and regimental crests. The Memorial Student Center displays an artist's rendition of Whiteley, a specimen, and the citation for the medal.

Capt. Eli Lamar Whiteley, Class of 1941, was the sixth Texas Aggie awarded the Medal of Honor.

WILLIAM GEORGE HARRELL

CLASS OF 1943

"Uncommon valor was a common virtue."

ADM. CHESTER W. NIMITZ

WILLIAM GEORGE HARRELL was born on June 26, 1922, in Rio Grande City, in the area of Texas commonly referred to as "the Valley." His parents were Roy E. and Hazel Marian Culber Harrell. His father was a former ranch hand and served in the cavalry during World War I. After the war he joined the Bureau of Immigration as a mounted officer patrolling the Mexican border, soon gaining a reputation for shootouts with *banditos* and "bootleggers." Harrell's father died in 1931, leaving his mother as the sole support of the family, including brother Dick, who was four years older, and sister Virginia, who was two years older.[1]

Young Harrell started grade school in Rio Grande City, then when the family moved to Mercedes, attended school there. He liked to hunt and camp and spent a lot of time with small boats on a nearby lake. He was a boy scout in junior high school and graduated from Mercedes High School in 1939. During the summer months, he worked at various odd jobs, including on a ranch one summer. Harrell inherited his father's love of horses and had two horses of his own. He was particularly interested in the scientific breeding of cattle and horses and wanted to attend Texas A&M to study agriculture. Applying for admission to the school, he requested animal husbandry as his field of study and cavalry as his required military-science course. Upon arrival on campus in September 1939, the five-foot-eight-and-a-half-inch, 128-pound freshman was assigned to Troop C, Cavalry. His sophomore year he was transferred to Troop D, Cavalry, the honor troop, and rode horses in all parades while the other cavalry units marched like infantry when parading at corps ceremonies.[2]

Harrell received some financial support from an aunt but knew that he had to help pay his own way through college. To ease his expenses, he requested to live in co-op housing. The co-op program came about during the depression, when self-reliant students who did not have the money for room and board in the regular college dormitories formed special residential groups. The students lived in what were called "project houses," where they did their own cooking, their own laundry, and anything else necessary. A project house contained about half the number of students as a regular dormitory company but roughly maintained the standard mix of classes and relationships between the classes as in the dormitories. The houses were self-governing just like the military units in the on-campus dormitories. At one time there were more than a thousand students living in the co-ops, many of them built or donated by A&M clubs and A&M mothers' clubs. Most of the residents had part-time jobs on campus or in the nearby community. Even though they did not live in the regular dormitories, the students were assigned to a corps unit and participated in corps activities.[3]

Living in co-op housing, there were times when Harrell would not know that the weekly drill or parade time had changed, and he would show up in the wrong uniform. His fellow troop members would be forced to quickly dress him in the correct uniform or hide him until after the drill session or parade was over.[4]

After completing four semesters at Texas A&M, Harrell left school to earn enough money to complete the last two years of his college education. When Pearl Harbor was bombed and the United States entered World War II, he decided to join the war effort. He tried to enlist in the army air corps twice but was rejected each time because of color blindness. He then tried to enlist in the navy and was again turned down. His next attempt to enlist was successful, when he was accepted by the Marine Corps in July 1942. After completing basic training at the Marine Corps Recruit Depot, San Diego, California, Harrell served in the depot's 1st Guard Company. He was then sent to Camp Elliott to train as an armorer. By the time he reported to Camp Pendleton for an assignment to Company A, 28th Marine Regiment, 5th Marine Division, he had been promoted to corporal.[5]

28TH MARINE REGIMENT

The 28th Marine Regiment was activated on February 8, 1944, at Camp Pendleton, California, as a part of the 5th Marine Division. It absorbed the remaining marines of the 1st Parachute Regiment, which had seen action in the Solomon Islands. The regiment also received hundreds of veterans of earlier campaigns, some in transit from combat areas in the Pacific, others from hospitals or from sick leave. These veteran officers and enlisted men brought with them combat experience and practical knowledge of the jungle and the Japanese foe. Other marines came from boot camps at Parris Island, South Carolina, and San Diego; training centers and schools; and ship-board detachments in the fleet.[6]

A marine regiment in 1945 was organized with a headquarters and service company, a weapons company, and three infantry battalions. The regiment, commanded by a colonel, was authorized 129 officers, eight warrant officers, and 3,044 enlisted men. It was also authorized U.S. Navy personnel to include two chaplains, two doctors, one dentist, and fourteen medical corpsmen. A battalion consisted of a headquarters company and three rifle companies. Commanded by a lieutenant colonel, the battalion comprised 35 officers and 877 enlisted men. It was also authorized U.S. Navy personnel to include two

doctors and forty medical corpsmen. The rifle company, commanded by a captain, comprised 7 officers and 247 enlisted men. It was authorized a company
headquarters, a machine-gun platoon, and three rifle platoons. The rifle platoon, commanded by a lieutenant, consisted of a headquarters and three rifle
squads. A rifle squad was led by a sergeant and had three fire teams of four men
each, for a total of thirteen marines. The weapons company had one 75-mm-
gun platoon, with four gun sections, and three 37-mm-gun platoons, with four
gun sections each. The company was commanded by a major and comprised
6 officers, one warrant officer, and 195 enlisted men. Gun platoons were commanded by lieutenants.[7]

The division training program directed that squad, platoon, company, battalion, and regimental training would follow in regular succession. The final
preparation for battle would consist of amphibious-assault exercises. The normal training period for the army and navy was five days a week, with the weekend or part of it off. The 5th Marine Division found that they could accomplish
more by training ten full days without a break, then take three days off.[8]

On September 18, 1944, the 28th shipped out of San Diego for Hawaii, landing at Hilo on the island of Hawaii (the "Big Island") on the twenty-fourth.
A new tent camp awaited at Camp Tarawa, located about sixty miles north of
Hilo on the leeward side of the island. It never rained on the Tarawa side, and
it was as dry as any desert.[9]

An intensive training program began after their arrival, with field problems involving flamethrower teams and demolition men. The marines trained
under live fire from artillery, mortars, and machine guns. Men scrambled up
steep slopes, rehearsing frontal attacks against mock pillboxes and bunkers.
The training featured thirty-mile forced marches with full combat packs and
weapons. It was a dawn-to-dusk schedule that sometimes went through the
night, all tailored to harden the men for Iwo Jima's wicked terrain and formidable defenses.

On January 7, 1945, the combat force departed Hilo for Pearl Harbor, where
the invasion fleet was being assembled. The fleet departed Pearl in late January
and, after stops to refuel at Eniwetok and Saipan, arrived in the Iwo Jima area.
Seventy-three mass-produced Liberty and Victory transports hauled the troops
and material.

The 5th Marine Division was assigned the area at the south end of the island
below Mount Suribachi. The 28th was one of four regiments to make the initial
landing and was assigned the left beach of the invasion area. The first objective
after securing the beachhead was to push inland and capture the airfield, then

to secure Mount Suribachi. (A group of marines from the 28th raised the flag on Mount Suribachi.) What was expected to be a campaign lasting three to four days turned into one lasting thirty-six days.

The 28th was ordered back to Hawaii with the division to recuperate, rebuild, and train for the next campaign, which all believed would be the invasion of Japan. Arriving in Hawaii on April 12, the marines returned to their tent city at Camp Tarawa. After an extensive liberty program, the regiment went to work overhauling equipment, absorbing replacements, and completing tactical and administrative reports. A stepped-up training program took into consideration the lessons learned on Iwo Jima, but because of the large number of replacements, it was necessary to start again with individual training.

Planning and training for Operation OLYMPIC — the invasion of Japan — continued during the summer of 1945. Battalion landing teams went through amphibious exercises at Maume Beach. The training served to build self-confidence and initiative in the men as well as teamwork in the unit.

After the surrender of Japan on August 14, the regiment shipped out to participate in the occupation. Landing in Sasebo on the island of Kyushu, the regiment placed guards on military installations and civilian centers such as the post office, the city hall, and police stations. The 28th ended its occupation duties in early December and boarded ships for the homeward trip to San Diego. By the end of the year, the regiment was back in its old area at Tent Camp 1, Camp Pendleton.

Late in January 1946 the 28th Marine Regiment was disbanded and passed into history. The regiment was awarded a Presidential Unit Citation for Iwo Jima.[10]

BATTLE OF IWO JIMA

Iwo Jima means "Sulphur Island" in Japanese and is one of the Volcano Islands east of Okinawa and about 700 miles south of Tokyo. The island is about 8.5 square miles in area and shaped like a pork chop. Its hilly, rocky, and generally barren terrain is dominated by Mount Suribachi, a 556-foot-high extinct volcano on the southern tip. The Japanese had fortified the island with a maze of concrete pillboxes, bunkers, shelters, and blockhouses that were capable of all-around defense and were mutually supporting. An elaborate cave system provided protected living spaces and sheltered the defensive artillery. The garrison consisted of more than 20,000 Japanese army and navy personnel and was commanded by Lt. Gen. Tadamichi Kuribayashi, a cavalry officer who had fought the Russians in the undeclared Russo-Japanese war of 1938–39. Kuribayashi's

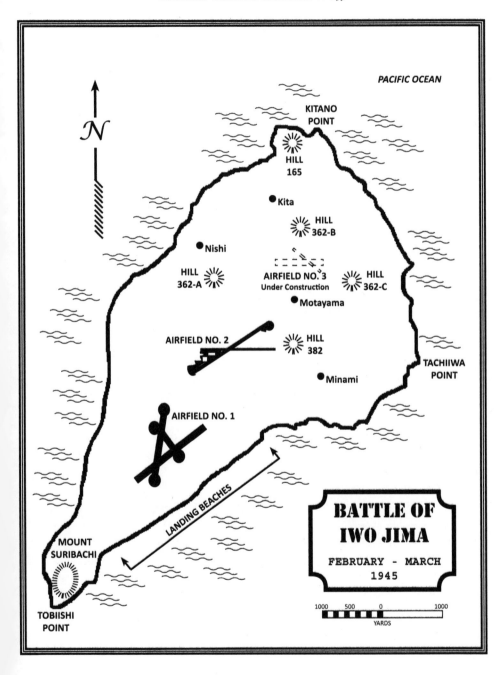

PACIFIC OCEAN

KITANO
POINT

HILL
165

Kita

HILL
362-B

Nishi

HILL
362-A

AIRFIELD NO. 3
Under Construction

HILL
362-C

Motayama

AIRFIELD NO. 2

HILL
382

Minami

TACHIIWA
POINT

AIRFIELD NO. 1

LANDING BEACHES

BATTLE OF
IWO JIMA

FEBRUARY - MARCH
1945

MOUNT
SURIBACHI

TOBIISHI
POINT

1000   500   0   1000
YARDS

plan for the island's defense was to allow the initial waves to land and, when the beaches were crowded with men and material, to unleash a heavy bombardment of mortar and artillery fire from Suribachi and the high ground in the north.[11]

Iwo Jima is halfway to Japan from the Marianas and sat squarely on the only direct route for the B-29 bombers in their campaign against the Japanese home islands. Iwo's primitive radar stations worked well enough to give interceptors time to take off, gain altitude, and ambush Japan-bound formations with devastating losses. Fierce fighter attacks and deadly antiaircraft fire, triggered by word of impending attacks flashed by wireless from the island, would again hit the Superfortresses when they made their bombing runs. Additionally, Japanese bombers from Iwo made raids on the airfields in the Marianas, causing considerable damage. But with the island's airfields in American hands, B-29s returning from raids with battle damage or low on fuel could have an emergency landing site available. The airfields could also be used for fighter aircraft to escort the bombers on their missions.[12]

The Japanese on Iwo Jima had been under periodic attacks by air and naval forces for several months. At 3 AM on D-day, February 19, the marines aboard the assault transports were roused from bunks by clanging gongs and loudspeakers blaring "Reveille, Reveille." A steak breakfast, the traditional meal before assaulting the beaches, was served to all hands. At 6:30 AM the order was given: "Land the landing force." The bombardment group of six battleships, five heavy cruisers, and ten destroyers began the pre-invasion shelling of the island as the first waves in their landing craft assembled in their designed areas. Three marine divisions (3rd, 4th, and 5th) were poised to assault Iwo Jima. The landing plan called for the 4th and 5th Divisions to land abreast at H-hour on D-day. The 3rd Division, in floating reserve, would land if and where needed.[13]

The daunting task of the first wave of AMTRACs (amphibious-assault vehicles) was to get ashore, smash any enemy positions they could find on the beach, grind fifty yards inland, and establish a defense perimeter for the landing force. No assault troops were in the seven-ton, steel-sided landing craft, only a three-man crew to drive it and fire its 75-mm howitzer and three machine guns. The first group landed at 9:02 AM and was followed by five waves of AMTRACs carrying the assault companies along with a wave of tank-carrying LCMs (landing-craft, mechanized). The landing force met only light resistance, the main problem encountered being the volcanic sand, which slowed the AMTRACs. The vehicles were stopped altogether, though, by the five- to eighteen-foot terraces directly inland. As soon as the AMTRACs stopped,

A wave of marines leaves the beach to drive inland against Japanese positions at the base of Mount Suribachi. Official U.S. Marine Corps Photo

troops leaped to the ground and immediately sank over their shoe tops in the loose, ashy soil.[14]

Opposition continued to be light until the attack had been carried inland about three hundred yards. At that point the invaders were deluged by mortar and artillery fire from Suribachi to the south and the high ground to the north. Heavy shells soon began to fall on the entire landing area, and the accuracy of this fire never varied as Japanese spotters looked down on the advancing Americans. The loose, slipping sand offered the pinned-down marines poor cover at best. Foxholes filled in almost as fast as a man could shovel.

By 10:35 AM on D-day, the 1st Battalion, 28th Marines had crossed Iwo Jima at its narrowest point just north of Suribachi, and their arrival at the western shore officially cut off Suribachi from the rest of the island. It took the rest of the day and bitter fighting to mop up the area to ensure that Suribachi stayed cut off. Behind the assault troops, follow-up units cleared bypassed pillboxes and other enemy emplacements. Tanks and artillery landed the afternoon of D-day and added their firepower to the assault.[15]

Once the island had been crossed, the 28th Marines turned south to seize Suribachi, while the other two regiments of the 5th Division turned north toward the two airfields and the main defenses. The 3rd Marine Division landed on D+3 and wedged into the line between the 4th and 5th Divisions. The 3rd moved inland to seize Airfield No. 1, and the 4th, on the right flank, turned north to attack Japanese positions along the eastern shore. By February 24 (D+5), Suribachi had been taken, though mopping-up actions continued. The lower third of the island was securely in the hands of the marines, and Airfield No. 1 was being readied to accommodate U.S. planes.

But the "Maginot Line" of Iwo Jima still lay ahead. Running across the entire width of the island and beginning at the foot of the Motoyama Plateau, the Japanese had established two major defensive lines manned by their best troops. The price of piercing and securing these double-tiered lines would be enormous. On February 27 (D+8) the 3rd Marine Division took Airfield No. 2, cracking the cross-island defense line in their sector. On March 1 (D+10) the 5th Marine Division advanced on the left (west) side of the island, with their assault forces weakened by mounting casualties. The 3rd Division continued to advance in the center, but the 4th Division on the right made little progress against fierce resistance. After twelve days of hard fighting, the conquered area of the island had undergone dramatic change. The navy began to unload supplies, and army garrison forces were beginning to arrive. The naval evacuation hospital and the army field hospital became operational, allowing casualties to receive medical care without the long delays caused by waiting for evacuation.[16]

On the night of March 2, Sergeant Harrell and Pfc. Andrew J. Carter, a nineteen-year-old from Paducah, Texas, shared a foxhole some twenty yards in advance of their company's command post. They took turns standing watch and sleeping, one hour on and one hour off. About five o'clock in the morning, Carter saw a number of shadowy figures coming toward him and fired four times with his M1 rifle, killing four Japanese soldiers. Harrell, who was catnapping, grabbed his carbine and killed two of the enemy as they emerged from a ravine under the light of a star shell. When Carter's rifle jammed, Harrell told him to return to the command post and get another. Making the trip in a hurry, he returned to see Harrell firing at some figures coming over a small hill. The Japanese threw several grenades, one of which landed in the foxhole and exploded. The explosion showered Harrell with volcanic sand and hot fragments, and he felt warm blood soaking his dungarees. As he attempted to rise, his left leg buckled under him. Harrell's left hand was almost severed, and his left arm dangled uselessly.

As Carter rejoined him, two Japanese lunged toward them. The first man swung his sword wildly. Carter pointed his weapon at him and pulled the trigger, but the weapon misfired. He then grabbed a Japanese rifle with bayonet that he had picked up the day before as a souvenir, and as the enemy soldier started over the edge of the foxhole, he virtually impaled him. Another enemy soldier, who later proved to be an officer, came at the position from another angle and slashed at Carter with a samurai sword. Carter threw up his left arm and suffered a nasty cut on his hand. Harrell, using his uninjured right hand, succeeded in drawing his .45-caliber pistol and shooting the officer. Sure that he was bleeding to death, the sergeant ordered Carter back to the command post. "There's no use both of us dying here." Carter said he was leaving, though only to go for help.

Slumped against the side of the foxhole, Harrell watched an enemy soldier jump in, landing not three feet from him. Another crouched beside the hole, and the two began talking, seemingly about him. When they realized the marine was alive, the one in the foxhole armed a grenade and set it next to Harrell's head. As the soldier climbed out, Harrell shot him dead. Still holding the .45 pistol in his remaining hand, he shoved the sputtering grenade toward the other enemy soldier. The grenade exploded, killing the enemy soldier, obliterating the pistol, and blowing off Harrell's right hand.

At dawn Harrell was evacuated from a position hedged by the bodies of twelve dead Japanese, at least five of whom he had personally killed in defense of the command post. His commander would later call the position the "two-man Alamo."

Carter recovered the sword that nearly claimed his life and sent it to Harrell's mother in Mercedes while he and Harrell were in the hospital in San Francisco. He was quoted as saying, "Bill deserved it more than I did." Carter was awarded the Navy Cross, and Harrell was awarded the Medal of Honor.[17]

By March 10 (D+19) the three divisions were closing on the north end of the island, but the enemy refused to capitulate. The 4th Division launched an all-out attack on March 19 (D+25) against the last pocket of resistance on the eastern side of the island, where the defenders fought back fiercely with rifles, hand grenades, and machine guns. The opposition became disorganized, and by midmorning the marines had completely overrun the pocket. Although an

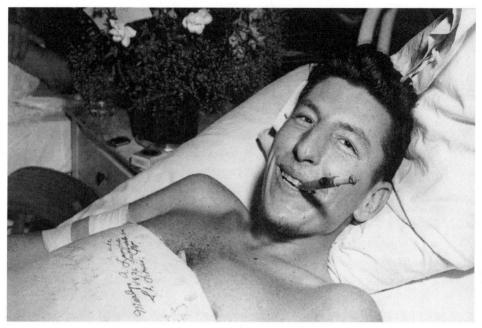

Sgt. William Harrell recovering from wounds with his signature cigarette holder.
Official U.S. Marine Corps Photo

estimated five hundred diehard enemy troops in a draw to the southwest of Kitano Point continued organized resistance, the high command chose this as the date to declare Iwo Jima officially in the hands of the United States. At 6:00 PM the battle was officially ended after twenty-six days and nine hours. For the next ten days, however, marines would continue to die as the enemy maintained their bitter resistance at Bloody Gorge. On the night of March 26 (D+35), a force of several hundred Japanese left their hiding places in by-passed caves and mounted an all-out attack on the newly arrived army-air-force units and the camp of the Seabees, inflicting death and destruction on the Americans.

It was not until the attackers reached the bivouac area of the 1st Pioneer Battalion that they encountered organized resistance. The battalion methodically slaughtered the oncoming horde, driving them back into the army-air-force bivouac area. Following in hot pursuit, members of the battalion overtook the survivors and quickly eliminated them.

Iwo Jima stands as the bloodiest battle in the history of the U.S. Marine

Corps. Marine casualties for the thirty-six days totaled 23,203 men, with 5,875 dead and 46 missing in action. In addition, 2,648 men were evacuated as combat fatigue casualties. Over 30 percent of the Marines killed in the Pacific War died on Iwo Jima.[18]

The marines took just 216 prisoners, many of them noncombatant Koreans from a labor battalion. During April and May, army forces occupying the island killed 1,602 Japanese in final mop-up operations and captured another 867. The total number of Japanese killed on Iwo Jima has been estimated at more than 20,000 men, or practically the entire garrison.[19]

AFTER IWO JIMA

Harrell's wounds were treated at the U.S. Army Hospital Station No. 369 on Iwo Jima, and he was later evacuated to the U.S. Naval Hospital No. 10 at Pearl Harbor. From Hawaii he was transferred to the U.S. Naval Hospital at Mare Island, California, for more treatment and rehabilitation.

On October 5, 1945, in a ceremony on the South Lawn of the White House, Pres. Harry S Truman presented the Medal of Honor to fourteen members of the navy and Marine Corps. Eight of the recipients, including Harrell, were survivors of the Iwo Jima battle. Truman said to those present: "They said we were soft, that we would not fight, that we could not win. We are not a warlike nation. We do not go to war for gain or territory; we go to war for principles, and we produce young men like these. I think I told every one of them that I would rather have that medal, the Congressional Medal of Honor, than be President of the United States."[20]

While recovering from his wounds at the Mare Island hospital in May 1945, Harrell met Larena Anderson, who was a clerical worker at the Mare Island Naval Base. The young female base employees were encouraged to visit the wounded in the base hospital for morale purposes. Larena and Harrell fell in love, and following his discharge from the Marine Corps, they were married on February 16, 1946, in the chapel on the Mare Island Naval Base. After the wedding Harrell and his new bride took the train to Mercedes, Texas. Back in his hometown, he was welcomed as a hero, and the local Kiwanis club joined with several other service groups to raise $25,000 for Harrell to buy a ranch. His friends in Mercedes encouraged him to return to A&M to complete his degree in animal husbandry, but when he was offered a job as a contact representative with the Veterans Administration, he moved to San Antonio and used the ranch funds to buy a house.

In 1947 his first son, William Carter, was born, his middle name to honor

Sgt. William Harrell receives the Medal of Honor from Pres. Harry S. Truman at the White House on October 5, 1945. Eleven marines received the nation's highest award at the ceremony. Official U.S. Marine Corps Photo by S.Sgt. Henry Rohland

Harrell's Iwo Jima foxhole comrade. William later followed in his father's footsteps by joining the Marine Corps and serving a combat tour in Vietnam. A daughter, Linda Gail, was born in 1948. After divorcing Larena, Harrell married Olive Cortese in 1951 and had two more children, Christie Lee, born in 1952, and Gary Douglas, born in 1953. Gary served in the U.S. Navy and retired with the rank of commander.

Harrell progressed from a contact representative to become chief of the Prosthetic Appliance Group at the Veterans Administration Center in San Antonio. He was later promoted to chief of the Prosthetics Division. He worked with amputees, blind, and deaf veterans and was a frequent speaker at service organizations and other civic groups, advocating for disabled veterans.

William Harrell receiving his discharge papers from the Marine Corps in 1946.
Courtesy Sam Houston Sanders Corps of Cadets Center, Texas A&M University

He organized a group of veterans who were amputees and called themselves the "Wrambling Wrecks." They built a clubhouse at Port Aransas and held an annual fishing tournament. Although he was equipped with general hooks for hands, Harrell was able to light a cigarette, use a telephone, drive, and take papers from the files at the VA office. He even designed a special device that allowed him to fire a pistol.[21]

TRAGIC DEATH OF A HERO

A story in the *San Antonio Express* of August 10, 1964, reported that Harrell and his friends, Ed and Geraldine Zumwalt, had been at an outdoor cookout at a mutual friend's house until about 10:30 PM on a Saturday night. About midnight, Zumwalt went to the Fort Sam Houston Officers Club and picked up his stepson, Norman Bolt, who worked in the club's kitchen. The youth said his father drove him home, and as they walked in the house, the phone was ringing. It was his mother calling, and she told him that she and Harrell had just arrived at the Harrell home. Norman said his father talked to his mother for about fifteen minutes and then left about 12:45 AM, saying that he was going to Harrell's home. He did not seem to be upset.

Harrell's wife, Olive, called her home about 3:15 AM from the San Antonio International Airport but received no answer. She and her two children had just returned from a five-week visit with relatives in New York City. After arriving at their home in a taxi, Harrell's ten-year-old son, Gary, discovered the body of his father on the lawn as he rushed up to the front door. A military carbine was lying about a foot away. Ed Zumwalt was lying in the driveway, and Geraldine Zumwalt was found in the kitchen.

The shootings had occurred sometime early Sunday morning. A neighbor reported hearing several shots about 1:30 or 2:00 AM. Dr. Ruben Santos, the medical examiner, ruled that Harrell had shot and killed the Zumwalts, then shot himself. Homicide detectives said they had no indication of any motive in the triple shooting. Santos said a motive "probably never will be established." Zumwalt, a gunsmith, was a veteran of the Korean War who had lost part of his left leg in combat. Friends said that he and Harrell met a year earlier and had been friends since then. Friends attending the cookout said there had been no signs of friction between Harrell and the couple.

Funeral services for Harrell were held on August 11, 1964, in the Georgian Chapel of the Porter Loring Funeral Home in San Antonio. Burial was in the Fort Sam Houston National Cemetery.[22]

No one knows what demons Harrell may have lived with after that terrible night on Iwo Jima. Perhaps he was as much a casualty as those who died on that bloody island nineteen years earlier.

HARRELL HONORS

The Junior Reserve Officer Training Corps building at the Mercedes High School is named for Harrell. A monument to him stands in downtown Mercedes, Texas. The Memorial Student Center on the campus of Texas A&M University displays an artist's rendition of Harrell, a specimen Medal of Honor, and the citation for the medal. A student dormitory at Texas A&M is named William G. Harrell Hall, and a large bronze bas-relief plaque hangs in the Sanders Corps of Cadets Center. Below the plaque is a display case containing Harrell's Medal of Honor, cadet insignia, photos, 5th Marine Division patch, Marine insignia, and a Japanese Samurai sword that is mentioned in the citation.

Sgt. William George Harrell, Class of 1943, was the seventh Texas Aggie awarded the Medal of Honor.

APPENDIX A

MEDAL OF HONOR CITATION
LLOYD HERBERT HUGHES JR.

★ ★ ★

Rank and organization: Second Lieutenant, 9th Air Force. *Place and date:* Ploesti Raid, Rumania, 1 August 1943. *Entered service at:* Corpus Christi, Tex. *Birth:* Alexandria, La. *G.O. No. :* 17, 26 February 1944. *Citation:* For conspicuous gallantry in action and intrepidity at the risk of his life above and beyond the call of duty. On 1 August 1943, Lieutenant Hughes served in the capacity of pilot of a heavy bombardment aircraft participating in a long and hazardous minimum-altitude attack against the Axis oil refineries of Ploesti, Rumania, launched from the northern shores of Africa. Flying in the last formation to attack the target, he arrived in the target area after previous flights had thoroughly alerted the enemy defenses. Approaching the target through intense and accurate antiaircraft fire and dense balloon barrages at dangerously low altitude, his plane received several direct hits from both large and small caliber antiaircraft guns which seriously damaged his aircraft, causing sheets of escaping gasoline to stream from the bomb bay and from the left wing. This damage was inflicted at a time prior to reaching the target when Lieutenant Hughes could have made a forced landing in any of the grain fields readily available at that time. The target area was blazing with burning oil tanks and damaged refinery installations from which flames leaped high above the bombing level of the formation. With full knowledge of the consequences of entering this blazing inferno when his airplane was profusely leaking gasoline in two separate locations, Lieutenant Hughes, motivated only by his high conception of duty which called for the destruction of his assigned target at any cost, did not elect to make a forced landing or turn back from the attack. Instead, rather than jeopardize the formation and the success of the attack, he unhesitatingly entered the blazing area and dropped his bomb load with great precision. After successfully bombing the objective, his aircraft emerged from the conflagration with the left wing aflame. Only then did he attempt a forced landing, but because of the advanced stage of the fire enveloping his aircraft, the plane crashed and was consumed. By Lieutenant Hughes' heroic decision to complete his mission regardless of the consequences in utter disregard of his own life, and by his gallant and valorous execution of this decision, he has rendered a service to our country in the defeat of our enemies which will everlastingly be outstanding in the annals of our Nation's history.

Author's note: Although the citation lists Hughes's unit as the Ninth Air Force, his bomb group was assigned to the Eighth Air Force and was on loan to the Ninth Air Force for Operation TIDAL WAVE. After the raid the Eighth Air Force units returned to England.

MEDAL OF HONOR CITATION
THOMAS WELDON FOWLER

★ ★ ★

Rank and organization: Second Lieutenant, 1st Armored Division. *Place and date:* Near Carano, Italy, 23 May 1944. *Entered service at:* Wichita Falls, Tex. *Birth:* Wichita Falls, Tex. *G.O. No. :* 84, 28 October 1944. *Citation:* For conspicuous gallantry and intrepidity at risk of life above and beyond the call of duty on 23 May 1944, in the vicinity of Carano, Italy. In the midst of a full-scale armored-infantry attack, Lieutenant Fowler, while on foot, came upon two completely disorganized infantry platoons held up in their advance by an enemy minefield. Although a tank officer, he immediately reorganized the infantry. He then made a personal reconnaissance through the minefield, clearing a path as he went, by lifting the antipersonnel mines out of the ground with his hands. After he had gone through the 75-yard belt of deadly explosives, he returned to the infantry and led them through the minefield, a squad at a time. As they deployed, Lieutenant Fowler, despite small-arms fire and the constant danger of antipersonnel mines, made a reconnaissance into enemy territory in search of a route to continue the advance. He then returned through the minefield and, on foot, he led the tanks through the mines into a position from which they could best support the infantry. Acting as scout 300 yards in front of the infantry, he led the two platoons forward until he had gained his objective, where he came upon several dug-in enemy infantrymen. Having taken them by surprise, Lieutenant Fowler dragged them out of their fox holes and sent them to the rear; twice, when they resisted, he threw hand grenades into their dugouts. Realizing that a dangerous gap existed between his company and the unit to his right, Lieutenant Fowler decided to continue his advance until the gap was filled. He reconnoitered to his front, brought the infantry into position where they dug in and, under heavy mortar and small-arms fire, brought his tanks forward. A few minutes later, the enemy began an armored counterattack. Several Mark IV tanks fired their cannons directly on Lieutenant Fowler's position. One of his tanks was set afire. With utter disregard for his own life, with shells bursting near him, he ran directly into the enemy tank fire to reach the burning vehicle. For one-half hour, under intense strafing from the advancing tanks, although all other elements had withdrawn, he remained in his forward position, attempting to save the lives of the wounded tank crew. Only when the enemy tanks had almost overrun him, did he withdraw a short distance where he personally rendered first aid to nine wounded infantrymen in the midst of the relentless incoming fire. Lieutenant Fowler's courage, his ability to estimate the situation and to recognize his full responsibility as an officer in the Army of the United States, exemplify the high traditions of the military service for which he later gave his life.

Author's note: Fowler was assigned to the 191st Tank Battalion, a separate battalion assigned to the U.S. Fifth Army. The listing of his unit as the 1st Armored Division was a mistake.

APPENDIX C

MEDAL OF HONOR CITATION

GEORGE DENNIS KEATHLEY

★ ★ ★

Rank and organization: Staff Sergeant, 85th Infantry Division. *Place and date:* Mt. Altuzzo, Italy, 14 September 1944. *Entered service at:* Lamesa, Tex. *Birth:* Olney, Tex. *G.O. No. :* 20, 29 March 1945. *Citation:* For conspicuous gallantry and intrepidity at risk of life above and beyond the call of duty, in action on the western ridge of Mount Altuzzo, Italy. After bitter fighting his company had advanced to within 50 yards of the objective, where it was held up due to intense enemy sniper, automatic, small-arms, and mortar fire. The enemy launched three desperate counterattacks in an effort to regain their former positions, but all three were repulsed with heavy casualties on both sides. All officers and noncommissioned officers of the Second and Third Platoons of Company B had become casualties and Staff Sergeant Keathley, guide of the First Platoon, moved up and assumed command of both the Second and Third Platoons, reduced to 20 men. The remnants of the two platoons were dangerously low on ammunition, so Staff Sergeant Keathley, under deadly small-arms and mortar fire, crawled from one casualty to another, collecting their ammunition and administering first aid. He then visited each man of his two platoons, issuing the precious ammunition he had collected from the dead and wounded, and giving them words of encouragement. The enemy now delivered their fourth counterattack, which was approximately two companies in strength. In a furious charge they attacked from the front and both flanks, throwing hand grenades, firing automatic weapons and assisted by a terrific mortar barrage. So strong was the enemy counterattack that the company was given up for lost. The remnants of the Second and Third Platoons of Company B were now looking to Staff Sergeant Keathley for leadership. He shouted his orders precisely and with determination and the men responded with all that was in them. Time after time the enemy tried to drive a wedge into Staff Sergeant Keathley's position and each time they were driven back, suffering huge casualties. Suddenly an enemy hand grenade hit and exploded near Staff Sergeant Keathley, inflicting a mortal wound to his left side. However, hurling defiance at the enemy, he rose to his feet. Taking his left hand away from his wound and using it to steady his rifle, he fired and killed an attacking enemy soldier, and continued shouting orders to his men. His heroic and intrepid action so inspired his men that they fought with incomparable determination and viciousness. For 15 minutes Staff Sergeant Keathley continued leading the men and effectively firing his rifle. He could have sought a sheltered spot and perhaps saved his life, but instead he elected to set an example for his men and make every possible effort to hold his position. Finally, friendly artillery fire helped force the enemy to withdraw, leaving behind many of their number either dead or seriously wounded. Staff Sergeant Keathley died a few moments later. Had it not been for his indomitable courage and incomparable heroism, the remnants of three rifle platoons of Company B might well have been annihilated by the overwhelming enemy attacking force. His actions were in keeping with the highest traditions of the military service.

MEDAL OF HONOR CITATION
HORACE SEAVER CARSWELL JR.

★ ★ ★

Rank and organization: Major, 308th Bombardment Group. *Place and date:* Over South China Sea, 26 October 1944. *Entered service at:* San Angelo, Tex. *Birth:* Fort Worth, Tex. *G.O. No. :* 14, 4 February 1946. *Citation:* He piloted a B-24 bomber in a one-plane strike against a Japanese convoy in the South China Sea on the night of 26 October 1944. Taking the enemy force of 12 ships escorted by at least two destroyers by surprise, he made one bombing run at 600 feet, scoring a near miss on one warship and escaping without drawing fire. He circled, and fully realizing that the convoy was thoroughly alerted and would meet his next attack with a barrage of antiaircraft fire, began a second low-level run which culminated in two direct hits on a large tanker. A hail of steel from Japanese guns riddled the bomber, knocking out two engines, damaging a third, crippling the hydraulic system, puncturing one gasoline tank, ripping uncounted holes in the aircraft, and wounding the copilot; but by magnificent display of flying skill, Major Carswell controlled the plane's plunge toward the sea and carefully forced it into a halting climb in the direction of the China shore. On reaching land, where it would have been possible to abandon the staggering bomber, one of the crew discovered that his parachute had been ripped by flak and rendered useless; the pilot, hoping to cross mountainous terrain and reach a base, continued onward until the third engine failed. He ordered the crew to bail out while he struggled to maintain altitude, and, refusing to save himself, chose to remain with his comrade and attempt a crash landing. He died when the airplane struck a mountainside and burned. With consummate gallantry and intrepidity, Major Carswell gave his life in a supreme effort to save all members of his crew. His sacrifice, far beyond that required of him, was in keeping with the traditional bravery of America's war heroes.

MEDAL OF HONOR CITATION
TURNEY WHITE LEONARD

★ ★ ★

Rank and organization: First Lieutenant, Company C, 893rd Tank Destroyer Battalion. *Place and date:* Kommerscheidt, Germany, 4–6 November 1944. *Entered service at:* Dallas, Tex. *Birth:* Dallas, Tex. *G.O. No. :* 74, 1 September 1945. *Citation:* He displayed extraordinary heroism while commanding a platoon of mobile weapons at Kommerscheidt, Germany, on 4, 5, and 6 November 1944. During the fierce 3-day engagement, he repeatedly braved overwhelming enemy fire in advance of his platoon to direct the fire of his tank destroyer from exposed dismounted positions. He went on lone reconnaissance missions to discover what opposition his men faced, and on one occasion, when fired upon by a hostile machinegun, advanced alone and eliminated the enemy emplacement with a hand grenade. When a strong German attack threatened to overrun friendly positions, he moved through withering artillery, mortar, and small-arms fire, reorganized confused infantry units whose leaders had become casualties, and exhorted them to hold firm. Although wounded early in battle, he continued to direct fire from his advanced position until he was disabled by a high-explosive shell which shattered his arm, forcing him to withdraw. He was last seen at a medical aid station which was subsequently captured by the enemy. By his superb courage, inspiring leadership, and indomitable fighting spirit, Lieutenant Leonard enabled our forces to hold off the enemy attack and was personally responsible for the direction of fire which destroyed six German tanks.

APPENDIX F

MEDAL OF HONOR CITATION

ELI LAMAR WHITELEY

★ ★ ★

Rank and organization: First Lieutenant, United States Army, Company L, 15th Infantry, 3rd Infantry Division. *Place and date:* Sigolsheim, France, 27 [*sic*] December 1944. *Entered service at:* Georgetown, Tex. *Birth:* Florence, Tex. *G.O. No. :* 79, 14 September 1945. *Citation:* While leading his platoon on 27 December 1944, in savage house-to-house fighting through the fortress town of Sigolsheim, France, he attacked a building through a street swept by withering mortar and automatic weapons fire. He was hit and severely wounded in the arm and shoulder; but he charged into the house alone and killed its two defenders. Hurling smoke and fragmentation grenades before him, he reached the next house and stormed inside killing 2 and capturing 11 of the enemy. He continued leading his platoon in the extremely dangerous task of clearing hostile troops from strong points along the street until he reached a building held by fanatical Nazi troops. Although suffering from wounds which had rendered his left arm useless, he advanced on this strongly defended house, and after blasting out a wall with bazooka fire, charged through a hail of bullets. Wedging his submachine gun under his uninjured arm, he rushed into the house through the hole torn by his rockets, killed 5 of the enemy and forced the remaining 12 to surrender. As he emerged to continue his fearless attack, he was again hit and critically wounded. In agony and with one eye pierced by a shell fragment, he shouted for his men to follow him to the next house. He was determined to stay in the fighting, and remained at the head of his platoon until forcibly evacuated. By his disregard for personal safety, his aggressiveness while suffering from severe wounds, his determined leadership and superb courage, Lieutenant Whiteley killed 9 Germans, captured 23 more and spearheaded an attack which cracked the core of enemy resistance in a vital area.

Author's note: Although the citation lists the date of the action as December 27, it actually took place on December 26.

MEDAL OF HONOR CITATION

WILLIAM GEORGE HARRELL

★ ★ ★

Rank and organization: Sergeant, United States Marine Corps, 1st Battalion, 28th Marines, 5th Marine Division. *Place and date:* Iwo Jima, Volcano Islands, 3 March 1945. *Entered service at:* Texas. *Birth:* Rio Grande City, Tex. *Citation:* For conspicuous gallantry and intrepidity at the risk of his life above and beyond the call of duty as leader of an assault group attached to the 1st Battalion, 28th Marines, 5th Marine Division during hand-to-hand combat with enemy Japanese at Iwo Jima, Volcano Islands, on 3 March 1945. Standing watch alternately with another marine in a terrain studded with caves and ravines, Sergeant Harrell was holding a position in a perimeter defense around the company command post when Japanese troops infiltrated our lines in the early hours of dawn. Awakened by a sudden attack, he quickly opened fire with his carbine and killed two of the enemy as they emerged from a ravine in the light of a star shell-burst. Unmindful of his danger as hostile grenades fell closer, he waged a fierce lone battle until an exploding missile tore off his left hand and fractured his thigh. He was vainly attempting to reload his carbine when his companion returned from the command post with another weapon. Wounded again by a Japanese who rushed the foxhole wielding a saber in the darkness, Sergeant Harrell succeeded in drawing his pistol and killing his opponent and then ordered his wounded companion to a place of safety. Exhausted by profuse bleeding but still unbeaten, he fearlessly met the challenge of two more enemy troops who charged his position and placed a grenade near his head. Killing one man with his pistol, he grasped the sputtering grenade with his good right hand and, pushing it painfully toward the crouching soldier, saw his remaining assailant destroyed but his own hand severed in the explosion. At dawn Sergeant Harrell was evacuated from a position hedged by the bodies of 12 dead Japanese, at least 5 of whom he had personally destroyed in his self-sacrificing defense of the command post. His grim fortitude, exceptional valor, and indomitable fighting spirit against almost insurmountable odds reflect the highest credit upon himself and enhance the finest traditions of the United States naval service.

NOTES
★ ★ ★

2. HISTORY OF THE MEDAL OF HONOR

1. U.S. Senate, Committee on Veterans' Affairs, *Medal of Honor Recipients, 1863–1973*, 93rd Cong., 1st sess., Oct. 22, 1973, S. Doc. 15, 1–4.

2. *Above and Beyond,* 5, 38–39, 71–72.

3. U.S. Senate, *Medal of Honor Recipients,* 4–5, 9–10.

4. *Above and Beyond,* 124.

5. Ibid., 203.

6. Ibid., 233.

7. Ibid., 246–48.

8. Ibid., 252–55, 264–65.

9. Ibid., 284–86.

10. Ibid., 286–87.

11. Ibid., 124.

12. "History of the Medal of Honor," Congressional Medal of Honor Society, http://www.cmohs.org/medal-history.php (accessed Sept. 26, 2009).

13. "Finally, Their Medals of Honor," *Houston Chronicle,* Jan. 11, 1997, 13A.

14. "World War II Heroes Recognized," *Houston Chronicle,* May 13, 2000, 4A.

15. "Medal of Honor," Theodore Roosevelt Association, http://www.theodoreroosevelt.org/life/medalofhonor.htm (accessed Oct. 15, 2009); U.S. Senate, *Medal of Honor Recipients,* 674–75.

16. *Above and Beyond,* 162.

17. Ibid., 161. The remains of the Vietnam Unknown Soldier were exhumed in 1998 and, based on DNA testing, was identified as those of air force lieutenant Joseph Blassie, who was shot down over An Loc in 1972. Afterward the crypt that once held Blassie's remains was replaced. The original inscription of "Vietnam" and the dates of that conflict were changed to "Honoring and Keeping Faith with America's Missing Servicemen" as a reminder of the commitment of the armed forces to make the fullest possible accounting of missing service members.

18. Ibid., 310.

3. LLOYD H. HUGHES

1. Rebecca Ann Jordan, "2nd Lt. Lloyd H. Hughes," Rajordan, http://www.rajordan.com/pete.

2. "Remembering Pete Hughes and His Band of Brothers," *Refugio County Press,* Dec. 15, 2007, 1.

3. Lloyd H. Hughes Jr., Application for Admission to The Agricultural and Mechanical College of Texas [hereinafter cited as Texas A&M], Sept. 14, 1939, Medal of Honor Collection, Texas A&M University Archives [hereinafter cited as MOHC, TAMU Archives; all documents cited are copies of the originals]; Jordan, "2nd Lt. Lloyd H. Hughes"; Ardery, *Bomber Pilot,* 44, 47; *Longhorn 1940* [TAMU yearbook], np.

4. Jordan, "2nd Lt. Lloyd H. Hughes."

5. Birdsall, *Log of the Liberators,* 309; Earl Cruickank, *The Ploesti Mission of 1 August 1943,* U.S. Air Force Historical Study 103 (Maxwell Air Force Base, Ala.: Air Force Historical Research Agency, June 1944), 34.

6. Ardery, *Bomber Pilot,* 59–60.

7. "389th BG Chronology," 389th Bomb Group, http://home.comcast.net/~skyscorpions/chrono.htm (Oct. 15, 2009), copy in MOHC, TAMU Archives.

8. Dugan and Stewart, *Ploesti,* 36, 44–45.

9. Colley, *Safely Rest,* 9–10.

10. Col. Harold L. James to family of Lloyd Hughes, Mar. 30, 2009, MOHC, TAMU Archives; Dugan and Stewart, *Ploesti,* 50.

11. "389th BG Chronology."

12. Brig. Gen. Uzal W. Ent, U.S. Army (Ret.), "Personality: Brigadier General Uzal G. Ent Commanded the American Bombers that Raided Ploesti in August 1943," *World War II* (Mar. 2000): 70.

13. Dugan and Stewart, *Ploesti,* 66.

14. Freeman, *Ploesti Raid,* 60.

15. Ronald Helder to Mr. and Mrs. Helder, July 31, 1943, MOHC, TAMU Archives.

16. Dugan and Stewart, *Ploesti,* 22.

17. Ent, "Personality," 70.

18. National Museum of the USAF, "Fact Sheet: Ploesti, Rumania," MOHC, TAMU Archives.

19. Dugan and Stewart, *Ploesti,* 180.

20. Ibid., 81, 83–85.

21. U.S. Senate, *Medal of Honor Recipients,* 584–85.

22. Maj. Gen. Philip Ardery, USAF (Ret.), "Perspectives: A Veteran of the August 1943 Ploesti Raid Reveals Long-hidden Details of the Costly Operation," *World War II* (July 2001): 84.

23. U.S. Senate, *Medal of Honor Recipients,* 584–85.

24. Dugan and Stewart, *Ploesti,* 187.

25. Ardery, *Bomber Pilot,* 104–106.

26. Headquarters, 389th Bomb Group (H), Army Air Forces, "Missing Air Crew Report 157," Aug. 2, 1943, MOHC, TAMU Archives; Freeman, *Ploesti Raid,* 153.

27. Ent, "Personality," 70; Cruickank, *Ploesti Mission,* 87–92, 103–105, 107.

28. Dugan and Stewart, *Ploesti,* 222.

29. Ibid., 224.

30. Ibid., 264, 276.

31. Philip Ardery to Norma Beasley, Jan. 24, 1992, MOHC, TAMU Archives.

32. Steere and Boardman, *Final Disposition of World War II Dead,* 258, 594, 654.

33. Jordan, "2nd Lt. Lloyd H. Hughes."

4. THOMAS W. FOWLER

1. Thomas W. Fowler, Application for Admission to Texas A&M, Aug. 25, 1939, MOHC, TAMU Archives; Thomas Fowler Jr., e-mail message to author, June 29, 2008, ibid.

2. Fowler, Application for Admission; Thomas Fowler Jr., interview by author, May 4, 2008, MOHC, TAMU Archives.

3. Perry, *Story of Texas A and M,* 233, 249.

4. Fowler interview, May 4, 2008.

5. *Longhorn 1940,* n.p.; *Longhorn 1941,* 321; *Longhorn 1942,* 337; *Longhorn 1943,* 86, 321.

6. Adams, *Keepers of the Spirit,* 150–53.

7. Fowler interview, May 4, 2008.

8. Ibid.

9. Tom Fowler to Mrs. Thomas Fowler, Mar. 8, 1944, MOHC, TAMU Archives.

10. Stanton, *Order of Battle,* 299.

11. *191st Tank Battalion* (Germany: N.p., [1945]), copy in MOHC, TAMU Archives; Stanton, *Order of Battle,* 299, 596.

12. Taggart, *Third Infantry Division,* 107; Atkinson, *Day of Battle,* 363.

13. Taggart, *Third Infantry Division,* 106–109.

14. U.S. Senate, *Medal of Honor Recipients,* 557; *191st Tank Battalion.*

15. Col. Floyd R. Waltz to Gen. John A Wicham Jr., June 8, 1984, with attached study, "Subject: Historical Record of the 191st Tank Battalion (Anzio and Rome-Arno Campaign)," MOHC, TAMU Archives, copy.

16. Oscar Smith, interview by author, Mar. 11, 2008, MOHC, TAMU Archives; Oscar Smith, interview by author, Mar. 30, 2008, ibid.; "Brave Texan Buried in Native Soil," *Fort Worth Star-Telegram,* July 28, 1948, 1.

17. Ralph Carr to Ann Fowler, July 18, 1944, MOHC, TAMU Archives.

18. Thomas Fowler Jr., interview by author, May 25, 2008, MOHC, TAMU Archives. Thomas Fowler Jr. graduated from Vanderbilt University in 1966 and served in the U.S. Navy as an ensign. He retired from a career as a stockbroker and lives in Denver, Colo.

19. Steere, *Graves Registration Service,* 81–84.

20. Steere and Boardman, *Final Disposition of World War II Dead,* 606–609.

21. Department of the Army, Individual Deceased Personnel File, MOHC, TAMU Archives; Fowler interview, May 25, 2008.

5. GEORGE D. KEATHLEY

1. William R. Hunt, "Olney, TX," Texas State Historical Association, The Handbook of Texas Online, http://www.tshaonline.org/handbook/online/articles/OO/hgo1.html.

2. Marlin Keathley, interview by author, Mar. 14, 2008, MOHC, TAMU Archives; George D. Keathley, Application for Admission to Texas A&M, Sept. 14, 1933, ibid.

3. *1934 Longhorn,* 87; *1935 Longhorn,* n.p.

4. James Kunkel, interview by author, Mar. 26, 2008, MOHC, TAMU Archives; Keathley interview.

5. "Lamesa Soldier Who Earned Highest Honor in Death, Died with Words of Love to Wife," *Lamesa Reporter-News,* Apr. 7, 1945, 1.

6. *Minturno to the Apennines* (Italy: Information-Education Section, Mediterranean Theater of Operations, U.S. Army, 1945), 2–3.

7. Ibid., 1–2.

8. War Department, "Table of Organization and Equipment No. 7-11," Feb. 26, 1944, MOHC, TAMU Archives.

9. *Minturno to the Apennines,* 3.

10. George Keathley to Mrs. W. C. Leberman [aunt], Apr. 2, 1944, MOHC, TAMU Archives.

11. *Minturno to the Apennines,* 4–20.

12. George Keathley to family, May 25, 1944, MOHC, TAMU Archives.

13. Headquarters, 85th Infantry Division, General Order 22, June 21, 1944, ibid., copy.

14. *Minturno to the Apennines,* 39.

15. George Keathley to family, June 6, 1944, MOHC, TAMU Archives.

16. *Minturno to the Apennines,* 43–44.

17. George Keathley to Katy Kay Keathley [niece], June 27, 1944, MOHC, TAMU Archives.

18. MacDonald and Mathews, *Three Battles,* 103–105, 107.

19. Ibid., 110–15.

20. Ibid., 132.

21. U.S. Senate, *Medal of Honor Recipients,* 593–94.

22. Gen. Mark Clark to Mrs. A. B. Vanarsdall, Jan. 30, 1945, MOHC, TAMU Archives.

23. Mrs. A. B. Vanarsdall to Gen. Mark Clark, Nov. 1, 1944, ibid.

24. Steere and Boardman, *Final Disposition of World War II Dead,* 603–605.

25. Kunkel interview; Carla Perry, interview by author, Apr. 24, 2008, MOHC, TAMU Archives.

26. "Nation Pays Eloquent Tribute to Texas Hero," *Fort Worth Star-Telegram,* Apr. 12, 1945, 1.

6. HORACE S. CARSWELL JR.

1. Horace S. Carswell Jr., Application for Admission to Texas A&M, July 12, 1934, MOHC, TAMU Archives; J'Nell L. Pate, "Carswell AFB's Major Horace S. Carswell, Jr., and His San Angelo Connection," *West Texas Historical Association Yearbook* 78 (2002): 64–70; *Longhorn 1935,* n.p.; *Horned Frog 1938* [Texas Christian University yearbook], 170, 188, 250; *Horned Frog 1939,* 178–79, 199, 222; *Horned Frog 1940,* 82–83, 103, 144.

2. Horace S. Carswell Jr., USAF Statement of Military Service, MOHC, TAMU Archives; Pate, "Carswell AFB's Major Horace S. Carswell," 65.

3. Carswell, Statement of Military Service.

4. Birdsall, *Log of the Liberators,* 164; Glines, *Chennault's Forgotten Warriors,* 44, 58.

5. Glines, *Chennault's Forgotten Warriors,* 248; "History," 308th Bombardment Group: China-Burma-India, 1942–1943, http://www.usaaf-in-cbi.com/308th_web/index.htm (accessed Oct. 19, 2009).

6. Glines, *Chennault's Forgotten Warriors,* 14.

7. Ibid., 18–20.

8. Ibid., 50; "History," 308th Bombardment Group.

9. Glines, *Chennault's Forgotten Warriors,* 249.

10. Ibid., 248–51; "Fort Worth Pilot Sank Jap Cruiser and Destroyer," *Fort Worth Star Telegram,* Oct. 18, 1944 (eve), 4.

11. Glines, *Chennault's Forgotten Warriors,* 257–58.

12. Ibid., 257–64.

13. Steere and Boardman, *Final Disposition of World War II Dead,* 428–32.

14. Pate, "Carswell AFB's Major Horace S. Carswell," 69; "Air Base Pays Tribute to Hero at Dedication," *Fort Worth Star-Telegram,* Oct. 18, 1986, 21.

15. "Baby Boy of Major Carswell Receives Medal of Honor for His Hero Father," *Fort Worth Star-Telegram,* Feb. 28, 1946, 1.

7. TURNEY W. LEONARD

1. Turney W. Leonard, Application for Admission to Texas A&M, June 26, 1938, MOHC, TAMU Archives; U.S. Census 1910, 1920, 1930.

2. Leonard, Application for Admission to Texas A&M.

3. Ibid.; James B. Hervey, interview by author, July 22, 2008, MOHC, TAMU Archives: Willard Worley, interview by author, July 22, 2008, ibid. Worley returned to Texas A&M after World War II and taught in the Electrical Engineering Department for thirty years.

4. Paul Wischkaemer to Calvin Boykin, Nov. 25, 1998, MOHC, TAMU Archives; Homer O. Gainer to Calvin Boykin, Nov. 12, 1998, ibid.; *Longhorn 1939,* n.p.; *Longhorn 1940,* n.p.; *Longhorn 1941,* 287; *Longhorn 1942,* 78, 303.

5. Gill, *Tank Destroyer Forces,* 12.

6. Stanton, *Order of Battle,* 338; Gabel, *Seek, Strike, and Destroy,* 45.

7. Stanton, *Order of Battle,* 338; Gill, *Tank Destroyer Forces,* 12, 165, 179, 183, 207, 230, 262.

8. Stanton, *Order of Battle,* 81–82.

9. Ibid., 89–91; MacDonald, *Siegfried Line,* 450–62.

10. Stanton, *Order of Battle,* 146–47; "History World War II," 78th Infantry Division WWII Living History Association, http://www.78thInfantry.org (accessed Oct. 15, 2009); Gavin, *On to Berlin,* 268.

11. Stanton, *Order of Battle,* 338; "History World War II," 78th Infantry Division.

12. Gill, *Tank Destroyer Forces,* 76–77.

13. Combat interview, Capt. Marion Pugh, Nov. 22, 1944, MOHC, TAMU Archives; Statement, S.Sgt. Marshall Pritts and Sgt. John Vitchook, Feb. 18, 1945, ibid.; Statement, Marion Pugh, Jan. 5, 1945, ibid.; MacDonald and Mathews, *Three Battles,* 251–54, 257, 300–301, 314–15, 323, 326, 348.

14. Lt. Col. Samuel E. Mays, Headquarters, 893rd Tank Destroyer Battalion, "Narrative of Unit Action October 28–November 9, 1944," Nov. 18, 1944, MOHC, TAMU Archives.

15. Ted Bullard, *Rhineland* (Washington, D.C.: Center for Military History, 1994), 18–22 (brochure); MacDonald and Mathews, *Three Battles,* 416–17.

16. Headquarters, 893rd Tank Destroyer Battalion, "Subject: Recommendation for Award," Jan. 5, 1945, MOHC, TAMU Archives; First Army Board Proceeding, Apr. 18, 1945, ibid.; "Hero's Mother to Receive Honor Medal," *Dallas Morning News,* Sept. 13, 1945, 13.

17. Information in this section is based on official documents and personal correspondence found in the Department of the Army's individual deceased personnel file for Turney W. Leonard. The file was obtained from the National Archives by Calvin C. Boykin Jr., Class of 1946, of College Station, Texas. Boykin served with a tank-destroyer battalion in Europe during World War II and was the president of the WWII Tank Destroyer Society.

18. Tyree Bell to QMG Memorial Division, May 5, 1947, MOHC, TAMU Archives.

19. Major General Witsell to Tyree Bell, Jan. 15, 1948, ibid.

20. Tyree Bell to Senator Connally, Jan. 2, 1948, ibid.; Quartermaster General to Senator Connally, Feb. 5, 1948, ibid.

21. U.S. Army, "Narrative of Investigations of Kommerscheidt, AGRC," Aug. 7, 1947, ibid.

22. U.S. Army, "Narrative of Investigation at Kommerscheidt, Germany, in September & October 1947, AGRC," ibid.

23. Letter, Department of the Army, Subject: Identification of Deceased, Aug. 9, 1948, ibid. The author was in the Huertgen Forest and Kommerscheidt in May 2007 and visited the site where the remains of an American soldier had been found five days earlier. As recently as October 2008 the remains of two 28th Division soldiers were discovered near Kommerscheidt.

24. War Department, "Battle Casualty Report," Aug. 15, 1949, MOHC, TAMU Archives.

25. Mrs. Leonard to AGRC, Oct. 1, 1949, ibid.

26. Richard Pierce to Casualty Section, AGO, May 8, 1949, ibid.

27. Lt. Col. Carl Peterson to Maj. Gen. Whitsell, adjutant general, Mar. 31, 1949, ibid.

28. Statement, Maj. Robert Haglett to Adjutant General, Apr. 5, 1949, ibid.

29. Statement, Herbert Dohman, Oct. 27, 1949, ibid.

30. Headquarters, AGRC, "Narrative of Investigation, Maj. R. E. Deppe," Nov. 2, 1949, ibid.

31. U.S. Army, Bremerhaven Port of Embarkation, Record of Transfer, May 6, 1950, ibid.

32. "Honors, Tributes Paid Fallen Hero," *Dallas Morning News,* May 31, 1950, 5.

33. Adams, *Keepers of the Spirit,* 74.

34. "A Special Aggie Ring Comes Home," *Texas Aggie,* Jan. 2001, 14–15.

8. ELI L. WHITELEY

1. Eli L. Whiteley, Application for Admission to Texas A&M, July 27, 1932, MOHC, TAMU Archives; Eli L. Whiteley, Application for Admission to Texas A&M, July 20, 1938, ibid.; *Longhorn 1939,* n.p.; *Longhorn 1940,* n.p.; *Longhorn 1941,* 98; Ruth Whiteley and Alice Wiese, interview by author, Sept. 22, 2008, MOHC, TAMU Archives.

2. "Orders Said 'Take It'–And Lt. Whiteley Did," *Dallas Morning News,* Sept. 9, 1962, 22; War Department, AGO form 66–1 (for Eli L. Whiteley), Feb. 1, 1942, MOHC, TAMU Archives.

3. Sawicki, *Infantry Regiments,* 82–84; Mahon and Romana, *Infantry Part I,* 100, 353–55.

4. Taggart, *Third Infantry Division,* 201, 217, 229.

5. Ibid., 237.

6. Ibid., 246, 276, 279.

7. Ibid., 291; *Dallas Morning News,* Sept. 9, 1962, 22.

8. Taggart, *Third Infantry Division,* 291, 293.

9. Headquarters, 15th Infantry Regiment, Subject: Recommendation for Award of Medal of Honor, Apr. 3, 1945, MOHC, TAMU Archives; U.S. Senate, *Medal of Honor Recipients,* 717.

10. Whiteley Medical Records, MOHC, TAMU Archives; "Heros of Aggieland to be Honored at Muster," *Bryan Eagle,* Apr. 20,1946, 1; Whiteley and Wiese interview; Alice Wiese, interview by author, Nov. 19, 2008, MOHC, TAMU Archives.

11. *Dallas Morning News,* Sept. 9, 1962, 22; Wiese interview.

12. Eli L. Whiteley, official transcript, Texas A&M, MOHC, TAMU Archives.

13. Murray Milford, interview by author, Oct. 6, 2008, MOHC, TAMU Archives.

14. Gene Bolton, interview by author, Oct. 10, 2008, ibid.

15. Whiteley and Wiese interview; "Medal of Honor Winner Laid to Rest," *The Eagle,* Dec. 6, 1986, 1.

16. Aggie Muster speech, Apr. 21, 1962, MOHC, TAMU Archives; background information provided by Jerry Cooper, Class of 1963, ibid.

17. Whiteley and Wiese interview.

18. "Medal of Honor Winner Laid to Rest," 1; "Funeral, Military Procession Set Today for Medal of Honor Recipient Whiteley," *The Battalion,* Dec. 5, 1986, 1.

9. WILLIAM G. HARRELL

1. "A Good Ol Boy," *Mid-Valley Town Crier,* May 28, 2008, 1.

2. William G. Harrell, Application for Admission to Texas A&M, July 8, 1939; Wells, *Fifty Marines,* 12; *Longhorn 1940,* n.p.

3. Harrell, Application for Admission; Perry, *Story of Texas A and M,* 96.

4. Wells, *Fifty Marines,* 12.

5. William Harrell, interview by author, Sept. 2, 2008, MOHC, TAMU Archives; Murphy, *Heroes of WWII,* 325.

6. Conner, *Spearhead,* 1.

7. Marine Corps Schools, "The Organization of the Marine Regiment," Mar. 27, 1944, MOHC, TAMU Archives.

8. Conner, *Spearhead,* 26; Wells, *Fifty Marines,* 96, 110–13.

9. Conner, *Spearhead,* 26; Ross, *Iwo Jima,* 26, 34.

10. Conner, *Spearhead,* 38, 125–30, 135, 174–76.

11. Ibid., 35, 47.

12. Ross, *Iwo Jima,* 14.

13. Conner, *Spearhead,* 36, 38.

14. Ross, *Iwo Jima,* 61.

15. Conner, *Spearhead,* 54.

16. Ibid., 77, 90; Ross, *Iwo Jima,* 183.

17. Allen, *First Battalion,* 130–31; U.S. Senate, *Medal of Honor Recipients,* 575–76; "A Good Ol Boy," 1.

18. Allen, *First Battalion,* 167, 194, 226; Connor, *Spearhead,* 119.

19. Ross, *Iwo Jima,* 341.

20. Harry S. Truman, "Remarks at the Presentation of the Congressional Medal of Honor to Fourteen Members of the Navy and Marine Corps," Harry Truman Library, MOHC, TAMU Archives.

21. *Texas Aggie,* Feb. 1963; "S.A. Medal of Honor Hero Kills Two, Ends Own Life," *San Antonio Express,* Aug. 10, 1964, 1; William Harrell interview; Gary Harrell, interview by author, Dec. 9, 2007; "Billy Harrell Is to Marry Navy Nurse," *Valley Morning Star,* Feb. 16, 1946, 2.

22. "S.A. Medal of Honor Hero Kills Two."

BIBLIOGRAPHY

★ ★ ★

Above and Beyond: A History of the Medal of Honor from the Civil War to Vietnam. Boston: Boston Publishing, 1985.

Adams, John Jr. *Keepers of the Spirit: The Corps of Cadets at Texas A&M 1876–2001.* College Station: Texas A&M University Press, 2001.

Allen, Robert E. *The First Battalion of the 28th Marines on Iwo Jima.* Jefferson, N.C.: McFarland, 1999.

Ardery, Philip. *Bomber Pilot: A Memoir of World War II.* Lexington: University Press of Kentucky, 1978.

Atkinson, Rick. *The Day of Battle: The War in Sicily and Italy, 1943–1944.* New York: Henry Holt, 2007.

Birdsall, Steve. *Log of the Liberators: An Illustrated History of the B-24.* New York: Doubleday, 1973.

Blumenson, Martin. *Mark Clark.* New York: Congdon and Weed, 1994.

———. *United States Army in World War II: Salerno to Cassino.* Washington, D.C.: GPO, 1969.

Boesch, Paul. *Road to Huertgen: Forest in Hell.* Houston: Gulf, 1962.

Boykin, Calvin C., Jr. *Gare la Bete.* College Station, Tex.: C&R, 1995.

Chennault, Claire Lee. *Way of a Fighter: The Memoirs of Claire Lee Chennault.* New York: G. P. Putnam's Sons, 1949.

Clarke, Jeffrey J., and Robert R. Smith. *United States Army in World War II: Riviera to the Rhine.* Washington, D.C.: GPO, 1993.

Colley, David. *Safely Rest.* New York: Berkley, 2004.

Conner, Howard M. *The Spearhead: The World War II History of the 5th Marine Division.* Washington, D.C.: Infantry Journal Press, 1950.

Currey, Cecil B. *Follow Me and Die: The Destruction of an American Division in World War II.* New York: Stein and Day, 1984.

Dethloff, Henry, with John Adams Jr. *Texas Aggies Go to War: In Service of Their Country.* College Station: Texas A&M University Press, 2006.

Dugan, James, and Carroll Stewart. *Ploesti: The Great Ground-Air Battle of 1 August 1943.* New York: Random House, 1962.

Ellis, John. *World War II: The Encyclopedia of Facts and Figures.* N.p.: Military Book Club, 1995.

Fisher, Ernest. *The United States Army in World War II: Cassino to the Alps.* Washington, D.C.: GPO, 1977.

Freeman, Roger A. *The Ploesti Raid: Through the Lens.* London: Church House, 2004.

Gabel, Christopher R. *Seek, Strike, and Destroy: U.S. Army Tank Destroyer Doctrine in World War II.* Fort Leavenworth, Kans.: GPO, 1985.

Gavin, James M. *On to Berlin: Battles of an Airborne Commander, 1943–1946.* New York: Viking, 1978.

Gill, Lonnie. *Tank Destroyer Forces, WWII.* Paducah, Ky.: Turner, 1992.

Glines, Carroll V. *Chennault's Forgotten Warriors: The Saga of the 308th Bomb Group in China.* Atglen, Pa.: Schiffer, 1995.

MacDonald, Charles B. *The Last Offensive.* Washington, D.C.: GPO, 1973.

———. *The Siegfried Line Campaign.* Washington, D.C.: GPO, 1963.

MacDonald, Charles B., and Sidney T. Mathews. *Three Battles: Arnaville, Altuzzo, and Schmidt.* Washington, D.C.: GPO, 1952.

Mahon, John K., and Danysh Romana. *Infantry Part I: Regular Army.* Army Lineage Series. Washington, D.C.: GPO, 1972.

Miller, Edward G. *A Dark and Bloody Ground: The Huertgen Forest and the Roer River Dams, 1944–1945.* College Station: Texas A&M University Press, 1995.

Murphy, Edward F. *Heroes of WWII.* New York: Ballantine, 1992.

Pate, J'Nell. *North of the River: A Brief History of North Fort Worth.* Fort Worth: TCU Press, 1994.

Perry, George S. *The Story of Texas A and M.* New York: McGraw-Hill, 1951.

Ross, Bill D. *Iwo Jima: Legacy of Valor.* New York: Vintage, 1986.

Sawicki, James A. *Infantry Regiments of the U.S. Army.* Dumbries, Va.: Wyvern, 1981.

———. *Tank Battalions of the U.S. Army.* Dumbries, Va.: Wyvern, 1983.

Stanton, Shelby L. *Order of Battle U.S. Army, World War II.* Novata, Calif.: Presidio, 1984.

Steere, Edward. *The Graves Registration Service in World War II.* Q.M.C. Historical Studies 21. Washington D.C.: GPO, 1951.

Steere, Edward, and Thayer M. Boardman. *Final Disposition of World War II Dead, 1945–51.* Washington, D.C.: GPO, 1957.

Taggart, Donald G. *History of the Third Infantry Division in World War II.* Nashville, Ky.: Battery, 1987.

U.S. Senate, Committee on Veterans' Affairs. *Medal of Honor Recipients, 1863–1973.* 93rd Cong., 1st sess., 1973. S. Doc. 15.

Wells, John K. *Give Me Fifty Marines Not Afraid to Die.* Abilene, Tex.: Quality Publications, 1995.

Whitlock, Flint. *The Rock of Anzio, from Sicily to Dachau: A History of the U.S. 45th Infantry Division.* Boulder, Colo.: Westview, 1998.

INDEX

★ ★ ★

Arnold, Henry H.: 26, 79
Association of Former Students: 106;
   directory of, 5, 91–92
Association of the U.S. Army: 106
Austin Grade School: 43
Australia: 16
Avignon, France: 120

B-17: 38
B-25: 81
B-24: 15, 27, 31, 38, 80; aircraft
   description, 24; crew composition,
   24; crew kit, 24; number produced,
   24
B-24J: aircraft description, 83
B-29: 134
Bari Airdrome: 27
Barker, Vernon: 18
Bartow, Dick: 21
Basel, Switzerland: 117
Basilone, John: 15
Battle of the Bulge: 95, 96, 101
Battalion, The: 124
Baugh, Sammy: 77
Belgium: 18
Bell, Martha H.: 91
Bell School: 111
Bell, Tyree: 91, 92, 101
Bell, Tyree Jr.: 91
Bengals, Matthias: 103
Benghazi, Libya: 27, 31, 37
Bennwihr, France: 117, 125
Berger, Denis: 7
Bergstein, Germany: 95, 100
Berka Four: 27
Besancon, France: 115
Biggs Field: 26, 77

Bloodworth, Morris: 123
Bloody Gorge: 138
Bolovan Cemetery: 37
Bolt, Norman: 141
Bolton, Gene: 123–24
Borglund, John: 21
Borglund, Will: 21
Bowen, Ray: 107–08
Boxer Rebellion: 113: Medals of Honor
   awarded, 14
Boy Scouts: 43
Brandenburg, Germany: 94
Brazos County Draft Board: 112
Bremerhaven, Germany: 105
British Air Aid Group (BAAG): mis-
   sion of, 85
British Units: 1st Infantry Division,
   49–50; 5th Infantry Division, 50;
   56th Infantry Division, 50
Brown, Lucy: 3
Brownell, Francis Edwin; 12
Bruce, Andrew D.: 92, 93
Bryan Air Force Base: 41
Bryan, Travis: 112
Buffalo Bill, see William F. Cody
Bulgaria: 37
Bureau of Immigration: 129
Bush, George H. W.: 18

C-123: 17
Caesar: 63
Cameron State School of Agriculture:
   57: 74
Camp Coxcomb: 59
Camp Custer: 59
Camp Dallas: 91
Camp Elliott: 130

Corps Units: Co. C, Infantry, 91; Co. G, Infantry, 23; Co. I, Infantry, 92; Headquarters Troop, Cavalry, 111; Troop B, Cavalry, 43, 76; Troop C, Cavalry, 129; Troop D, Cavalry, 57, 129
Corpus Christi Junior College (Del Mar College): 23, 41
Corregidor, Philippines: 80
Cortese, Olive. *See* Harrell, Olive Cortese
Creditul Minier: 37
Crestview Memorial Park: 55
Criswell, Benjamin: 13
Crozier Technical High School. *See* Dallas Technical School
Custer, George A.: 13
Custer, Tom: 13
Cyprus: 37
Czechoslovakia: 18

Dachau, Germany: 48
Dallas Technical School: 91, 105
Dalton, Malcolm C.: 36
Davis-Monthan Field: 26, 79
Dean, William F.: 16
Denver Avenue Grade School: 76
Deppe, R. E.: 105
Desert Training Center: 48, 59
Dibble Army Hospital: 122
Distinguished Service Cross: 37, 84
Distinguished Unit Citation: 80
Distribution Centers: 40, 55
Dolman, Hubert: 104–105
Donaldson, Charles K.: 120
Donlon, Roger H. C.: 16–17
Doolittle, Jimmy: 15
Dozier, Charles J.: 69

Driscoll, Robert C.: 104–05
Duncan Hall: 92
Duren, Germany: 96

East China: 80
Eastside Church of Christ: 6
Edison Community College: 3
893rd Tank Destroyer Battalion: 1, 98,109; award of Belgium Croix de Guerre to, 95; campaign credits, 96; landing at Normandy, 94; liberation of Paris, 94; losses at Kommerscheidt, 100; organization of, 93
8th Service Command: 101
Eisenhower, Dwight D.: 27, 122
Ellison, Charles D.: 105
Ellsworth, E. E.: 12
Elmendorf Air Force Base: 89
Eniwetok: 131
Ent, Uzal G.: 27, 32
Ewing, Hazel. *See* Hughes, Hazel Ewing
Ewing, Sharon: 5

Fannin Grade School: 91
Fedela, Morocco: 114
1st Guard Company: 130
51st General Hospital: 120
First Armored Division Museum: 7
Fisher, Bruce: 126
Florence, Italy: 65, 70
Flying Training Command: 38
Florence American Military Cemetery: description of, 70; burials in, 70
Flying Tigers. *See* American Volunteer Group
Formosa: 83
Formosa Strait: 80